Greece, Turkey, NATO and the Cyprus Issue 1973–1988

This volume examines one of the most sensitive issues in the contemporary diplomatic history of the eastern Mediterranean, namely, the nexus between Greece, Turkey, the Cyprus problem and NATO in the crucial period between 1973 and 1988. This time span begins with the emergence of the Aegean dispute in 1973 and ends with the most comprehensive attempt to date to solve the Greek–Turkish conflict in the wake of the Davos rapprochement process in 1988. Due to the formation of all subsequent legal, geopolitical and geoeconomic facets of this complex relationship, this period was the most crucial in the development of the Greek–Turkish conflict. This period also coincided with some serious crises within the North Atlantic alliance that, as a result of the ruthless rivalry between two of its members, rocked the very foundations of the organization's most vulnerable and sensitive southern flank. The Cyprus issue and the many hermeneutic approaches deployed about the 1974 war are also critically re-examined, and for that purpose, the analysis in this book goes back to developments that occurred in the first half of the 20th century.

This volume, which has been meticulously researched, will be of interest to those studying the recent history and politics of Greece, Turkey and Cyprus, as well as to researchers with an interest in regional and international relations, and conflict studies.

Andreas Stergiou is Professor of European History and Politics, Department of Economics, University of Thessaly, Greece.

Europa Regional Perspectives

Providing in-depth analysis with a global reach, this series from Europa examines a wide range of contemporary political, economic, developmental and social issues in regional perspective. Intended to complement the Europa Regional Surveys of the World series, Europa Regional Perspectives will be a valuable resource for academics, students, researchers, policymakers, business people and anyone with an interest in current world affairs with an emphasis on regional issues.

While the Europa World Year Book and its associated Regional Surveys inform on and analyse contemporary economic, political and social developments, the Editors considered the need for more in-depth volumes written and/or edited by specialists in their field, in order to delve into particular regional situations. Volumes in the series are not constrained by any particular template, but may explore recent political, economic, international relations, social, defence, or other issues in order to increase knowledge. Regions are thus not specifically defined, and volumes may focus on small or large groups of countries, regions or blocs.

Social Welfare Issues in Southern Europe
Edited by Maria Brown and Michael Briguglio

Catalonia, Scotland and the EU
Visions of Independence and Integration
Niklas Bremberg and Richard Gillespie

Constructive Competition in the Caspian Sea Region?
An Alternative Image
Agha Bayramov

Central Asia's Economic Rebirth in the Shadow of the New Great Game
Djoomart Otorbaev

The Nordic, Baltic and Visegrád Small Powers in Europe
A Dance with Giants for Survival and Prosperity
Hilmar Þór Hilmarsson

For more information about this series, please visit: www.routledge.com/Europa-Regional-Perspectives/book-series/ERP.

Greece, Turkey, NATO and the Cyprus Issue 1973–1988

Enemies Allied

Andreas Stergiou

Routledge
Taylor & Francis Group

LONDON AND NEW YORK

First published 2024
by Routledge
4 Park Square, Milton Park, Abingdon, Oxon OX14 4RN

and by Routledge
605 Third Avenue, New York, NY 10158

Routledge is an imprint of the Taylor & Francis Group, an informa business

© 2024 Andreas Stergiou

The right of Andreas Stergiou to be identified as author of this work has been asserted in accordance with sections 77 and 78 of the Copyright, Designs and Patents Act 1988.

British Library Cataloguing in Publication Data
A catalogue record for this book is available from the British Library

Library of Congress Cataloging-in-Publication Data
A catalog record has been requested for this book

ISBN: 978-1-032-39503-6 (hbk)
ISBN: 978-1-032-39506-7 (pbk)
ISBN: 978-1-003-35003-3 (ebk)

DOI: 10.4324/9781003350033

Typeset in Times New Roman
by Taylor & Francis Books

To my brothers Sergio, Apostolidi and Michali Zouboulaki

Contents

Acknowledgements

The task of compiling this book has been a meticulous, solitary and highly explorative voyage that lasted longer than two years. Reaching the end of this voyage, I wish to thank all those who have supported my efforts for the realisation of this book by offering multi-faceted assistance. First of all, I would like to thank Lia Largaespada Molina, Archives Clerk in the NATO Archives for her valuable assistance. Second, I would like to mention my gratefulness to the colleagues and friends Dionyssis Chourchoulis, Argyris Tassoulas and Lykourgos Kourkouvelas for their multi-faceted assistance. Finally, I would like to thank Cathy Hartley and Martin Pettitt from the Routledge staff for embracing the project, supporting my efforts and giving me the opportunity to publish this Focus volume putting across a tight and condensed overview of this complex topic.

Abbreviations

CINCSOUTH	Commander-in-Chief, Allied Forces Southern Europe
EC	European Community
ELDYK	Greek Cyprus Force
FIR	Flight Information Region
ICAO	International Civil Aviation Organization
NARA	National Archives and Records Administration
NATO	North Atlantic Treaty Organization
PASOK (Party)	Panhellenic Socialist Movement
SACEUR	The Supreme Allied Commander Europe
TRNC	Turkish Republic of Northern Cyprus
TURDYK	Turkish Cyprus Force

Introduction

This book touches upon one of the most sensitive issues in the contemporary diplomatic history of the eastern Mediterranean, the nexus between Greece and Turkey, the Cyprus problem and NATO in the crucial period between 1973–1989. This time span begins with the emergence of the Aegean dispute in 1973 and ends with the most comprehensive so far attempt to solve the Greek–Turkish conflict in the wake of the Davos rapprochement process in 1988. Due to the formation of all subsequent legal, geopolitical and geoeconomic facets of this complex relationship, the aforementioned time is the most crucial in the development of the Greek–Turkish conflict. This period of time also coincides with some serious crises within the North-Atlantic alliance that, as a result of the ruthless rivalry between two of its members, rocked the very foundations of the alliance's most vulnerable and sensitive southern flank. The Cyprus issue and the many hermeneutic strategies used in the 1974 war are also critically re-examined at the same time. For that purpose, the analysis goes back to developments that occurred in the first half of the 20th century.

Both Greece's and Turkey's accession to NATO in February 1952 had been hailed as a great accomplishment, since NATO membership offered a shield against a feared Soviet Bloc aggression, generated hopes for additional military and financial aid, and tied Greece and Turkey to the West (Chourchoulis & Kourkouvelas, 2012, p. 497; Athanasopoulou, 1999, pp. 416–417). Although in the following years various crises in Greek-Turkish relations or in Greece-Balkan relations occurred, NATO credibility was never seriously doubted by Athens. NATO membership continued to be a major manifestation of Greece's Western identity, and a pillar of Greek security (Hatzivassiliou, 2006). This all was to change in 1974, in the *annus mirabilis* of the contemporary history of international relations in the eastern Mediterranean.

DOI: 10.4324/9781003350033-1

In the period between 1967–1974 of the Greek dictatorship, the military regime in Athens was treated by NATO with leniency, although the alliance was not content with the junta's practices. However, as it had been the case with Spain and Portugal as well, the need to safeguard itself against the potential threat the Soviets were posing in the Mediterranean transcended any moral considerations (Maragkou, 2009, p. 363).

Ardent speculations about the existence of hydrocarbons in the Aegean during the first big energy crisis in 1973 triggered a staggeringly broad sequence of events that brought the two countries to the verge of war. Moreover, 1973 signals in essence the advent of the Aegean dispute. At that time, Turkey started questioning the legal status of the Aegean Sea seeking a different arrangement that, in Ankara's opinion, could protect Turkey's vital interests in the region and prevent Greeks from turning the Aegean Sea into a Greek lake.

The main bulk of the interrelated controversies over sovereignty and related rights in the region (the delimitation of territorial waters, of national airspace, of exclusive economic zones, of the continental shelf, the role of flight information regions (FIR)) for the control of military flight activity and the issue of the demilitarised status assigned to some of the Greek islands in the region, was more or less formed between 1973 and 1976.[1]

The Cyprus conflict had been simmering for quite some time from 1955 onwards and sometimes boiled over into organised or spontaneous violence. The seeds of division, however, between the two communities existed a long time ago before the openly violent acts occurred, as a result of the Greek and Turkish nationalism instilled in Greek and Turkish Cypriots in many ways. The termination of the British colonial rule and the establishment of the Cyprus Republic compounded the divisive tendencies, causing continuous tensions not only between the two ethnical communities but also within Greek Cypriot society. The accumulated tensions culminated in 1974. On 15 July 1974, forces of the Cypriot National Guard and other pro-*Enosis*, i.e. union with Greece, forces under direct instructions from Greece carried out a military coup against the legitimate President of the Republic of Cyprus, Makarios. The coup was swiftly followed by the Turkish invasion of Cyprus on 20 July with the aim of ousting the puppet regime[2] and restoring the political status quo ante. Surprisingly, this took the military brass in Athens completely by surprise, revealing its inability to provide military assistance to Cyprus and to address the crisis. But soon, the invasion[3] spread over the whole northern part of the island. A series of crucial decisions by the military regime in Athens in the 72 hours after the Turkish invasion signalled the collapse of the authoritarian rule and paved the way for the surrender of power to a civilian government. On 23 July, finding themselves under enormous pressure, both the dictatorship in Athens and the puppet regime in Nicosia collapsed, and two days later formal peace talks began in Geneva between Greece, Turkey and the UK.

In mid-August 1974, and while another round of discussions was being held in Geneva, Turkey surprisingly resumed its offensive, this time extending its occupation over about 37% of the island. Two days later, the UN Security Council recorded "its formal disapproval of the unilateral military actions undertaken against the Republic of Cyprus". This invasion was accompanied by mass executions of hundreds of civilians and war prisoners, rapes and ill-treatment of captives, while most of the Greek-Cypriot inhabitants (approximately 180,000) were forced to flee towards the south. In the southern part of the island, Turkish Cypriots were also exposed to violent reprisals and approximately 50,000 had also to flee, either towards the north or to the British military bases. To put it plainly, a large-scale ethnic cleansing occurred and, when the ceasefire was eventually declared, the island had been partitioned along ethnic lines and 1,600 Greek Cypriots had gone missing. Within a month, a 400-year-long coexistence between two ethnic Cypriot communities was ruined (Attalides, 2003, pp. 162–179).

In any case, after the second phase of the Turkish invasion, Athens withdrew from the military structure of the alliance, in a move that from one point of view looked very courageous and from another very impetuous. Athens probably hoped that such a gesture would cause NATO to put pressure on Turkey to change its course in Cyprus, neglecting at the given time other practical consequences for Greek security. The new democratic Karamanlis-led government, however, was faced with a strong tide of popular emotion against NATO.

For this reason, fierce anti-American and often slightly pro-Soviet propaganda in the post-dictatorial era[4] in Greece and Cyprus suggested NATO's complicity in the Turkish invasion and occupation of Northern Cyprus. This is certainly an exaggerated assumption. It would have been complicated for NATO to turn against a member such as Turkey, for something it did to a non-member such as Cyprus. However, the danger of a high-scale Greek–Turkish war should have galvanised the North-Atlantic alliance and moved NATO to engage in actions that would de-escalate the crisis. NATO did not do that and remained conspicuously indifferent during the whole crisis. However, as will be shown in the study, Greece confronted the cynical indifference of their NATO allies at a crucial time. And yet, in the years before NATO Secretary General's reports (watching briefs) on the Greek–Turkish relations underscored that any weakening in the cohesion, and solidarity of the alliance as a whole by a deterioration of the relations of two of its members in the eastern Mediterranean should be avoided at all costs.[5] Furthermore, in his report of 1972, General Secretary Joseph Lunz pointed out in regard to Cyprus that because of its highly positive implications for the southern flank of the alliance, it constituted a precious affirmation of the allied will for solidarity in the sector of the eastern Mediterranean where the situation continued to give cause for concern.[6] Nonetheless, at the most crucial moment NATO remained inert and silent.

As the Greek Prime Minister Konstantinos Karamanlis himself pointed out in his letter to all leaders of the NATO countries after Greece's withdrawal from NATO, *fundamental provisions of the North Atlantic Treaty regulating relations between the member states and requiring them to resort to peaceful means to settle their disputes, were disregarded. The Declaration on Atlantic Relations, signed in Brussels in June 1974, was denounced. Finally, the consultation process between the allies was de facto abolished. Furthermore, in the wake of the Turkish invasion, weapons intended for common defence were used to attack an independent UN member state.* [7]

The decisive role of the US Secretary of State Henry Kissinger and especially his pro-Turkish stance[8] and especially in the conspicuous absence of the North-Atlantic alliance during the Cyprus crisis in the Summer of 1974 has been emphasised by many scholars. Why did Kissinger not oppose a Turkish landing as President Johnson had in 1964 and 1967? As other scholars have also pointed out, it is particularly ironic that Kissinger did not even try for a peace based on *Realpolitik*, that is, a peace based on balance of power, and did not foresee what actually happened: 40% of Cyprus under Turkish occupation, a divided republic flooded with refugees bitter enmity toward the United States from all sides, and disarray on NATO's eastern flank (Camp, 1980, p. 58).

Against this background, a short time after the dramatic events, the political and military leadership in Athens and in Ankara began rearranging foreign policy priorities, as the conventional Cold War doctrine against a possible Communist attack appeared outdated. Greece could not rely on NATO as a security provider either, while Turkey was faced with a US arms embargo. Moreover, from the autumn of 1974 onwards, Turkey started challenging the long-standing practices and the existing legal status in the Aegean Sea: Greece's claimed continental shelf, Greece's mineral exploration rights, Athens's control of the Aegean Flight Information Region, etc.[9]

In any case, Greece had to seek alternatives and renegotiate its position in the alliance, presumably in the form of a different relationship with NATO, with which Athens began negotiating again a few years later. The negotiations and deliberations on the reintegration of Greece turned out to be thorny and time-consuming, because Athens and Ankara alternately vetoed or rejected NATO-mediated proposals. It was not before the fall of 1980 and only after the military coup d'état in Turkey that the Turkish military accepted Greece's reintegration in a bid to reduce domestic problems and foreign policy problems on other fronts.

Greece's return to NATO did not herald by any means the inauguration of an era of peace and tranquillity in the eastern Mediterranean. Turkey's dictatorial regime resorted to many maverick actions in its external relations, while the Greek idiosyncratic socialism prevailing in the country for the whole 1980s was associated with a strong nationalistic, anti-Turkish, anti-Western, i.e. anti-NATO, anti-American and anti-European rhetoric. As a result, the 1981–1988 period was beset with increasing tensions between Turkey, Greece and Cyprus, where the occupied territory declared itself as a state. It was a time of utter despair for the North-Atlantic alliance and the Western camp due to the permanent fear of an imminent collapse of NATO's south-east flank amidst a rekindled Cold War and widespread geopolitical uncertainty in the region.

In order to maintain stability in the south-east wing of the alliance, the NATO countries followed an unorthodox course in the Greek–Turkish–Cyprus conflict. Although they had a well-shaped and clear legal opinion about various aspects and layers of the conflict, such as the militarisation of the eastern Aegean islands, they preferred to suppress it and not to divulge it publicly out of fear that the conflicting parties would use it against each other, thereby omitting at the same time to show gratefulness to them. This turned out to backfire. The conflicting parties entrenched themselves in their positions, and perceived their allies' silence as consent for their deeds increasing the potential for conflict. Thus, it was only a matter of time before the tension escalated again into a serious crisis, as happened in 1987, when the two sides came literally to the brink of war.

The study intends to get to the bottom of all these developments, whose reverberations are still haunting the region, by using extensive primary sources from various countries: Greece (archive of Konstantinos Karamanlis,[10] archive of Evangelos Averof[11], Konstantinos

Papakonstantinou[12] Archive in the Konstantinos G. Karamanlis Foundation Athens, Greece), the Republic of Cyprus (state archive), the NATO Archive, the United States (National Archives and Records Administration cited as NARA, Dwight Eisenhower Library Archives, CIA Releases, Wikileaks Releases, Department of State Releases), the Archive of the Foreign Ministry of Former East Germany, the Political Archive of the Federal German Foreign Ministry, the Cyprus State Archives (Archive of the Foreign Ministry), the United Kingdom (Public Record Office), as well as the State Archive of Israel. It should be noted that the British archives are of great importance for the period under examination not only because of the traditional British interests in the eastern Mediterranean but also due to the term of Lord Carrington as Secretary General of NATO from June 1984 until July 1988. Lord Carrington who had previously served as Secretary of State for Defence, upheld close ties with the Foreign Office during his service as NATO Secretary General, because, among other reasons, the other Western European states were promoting at the same time their own European Defence System without London's compliance. The study also draws information from the series of primary sources gathered by the Hellenic Parliament and the House Representatives of Cyprus known as *Fakelos tis Kyprou* (The Cyprus File) which has been published in separate volumes from 2018 to date.

Notes

1 For a detailed analysis of the legal parameters of the Greek–Turkish maritime dispute, see Stergiou, 2022.
2 Some authors believe that the military coup just provided the Turks with the pretext to invade (Couloumbis, 1996, pp. 80–84)
3 In Turkish official historiography the invasion is touted euphemistically "Peace Operation".
4 Anti-Americanism had occurred in Greece earlier. After World War II, it was confined to the Greek Communist Party and later to the political forces of the political centre and the democratic left. This was relied on a critique of American policies supporting dictatorships while the US formally espoused the ideals of liberty. In the post-1974 anti-Americanism largely coincides with the critique on US policy towards the Greek military junta and the political rise of the Greek Socialist party and its leader, the US citizen and former professor at the Berkeley University Andreas Papandreou. Papandreou gradually transformed anti-Americanism from a reaction to what the US did in and towards Greece to basic component of Greek nationalism (Stivachtis, 2010, pp. 63–71).
5 NATO archive: Document PO /70/522: "Secretary General's Greek-Turkish Relations Watching Brief, 23 November 1970"; PO 71/658: "Secretary General's Greek-Turkish relations Watching Brief 29 November 1971".

6 See an example in NATO Archive: Document PO 72/422 (Revised): "Report of the NATO Secretary General on the Watching Brief to the Ministerial Meeting of December 1972, 29 November 1972".

7 *Konstantinos Karamanlis Archive 2005. Gegonota kai Keimena* [Events and texts], vol. 8., pp. 131–133.

8 Kissinger's bias and favoritism toward Turkey are also confirmed underscored by US diplomats (see Library of Congress. The Association for Diplomatic Studies and Training Foreign Affairs Oral History Project, Interview with US Ambassador in Ankara 1977–1980 Ronald I. Spiers. http://www.loc.gov/item/mfdipbib001109) and many authors: Ignantiou-Venizelos (Ignatiou & Venezelos, 2002), Sotiris Rizas (Rizas, 2018, pp. 103–104) and Mallinson (2016).

9 On 4 August 1974, the Turkish government issued the notorious NOTAM 714 requiring all aircraft approaching Turkish airspace to report their position and flight plan on reaching the Aegean median line with the alleged purpose to distinguish between innocent flights and potential attackers bound for targets to Asia Minor (Bahcheli, 1990, p. 144).

10 Prime Minister of Greece, 1974–1989 and President of the Hellenic Republic, 1980–1985

11 Greece's Defence Minister, 1974–1981.

12 Minister of Justice, July–October 1974, President of the Hellenic Parliament, 1974–1977.

References

Primary sources

NATO Archive

Foreign Relations of the United States, 1969–1976, Volume XXIX, Eastern Mediterranean, 1969–1972 (cited as FRUS). US Department of State Office of the Historian, Bureau of Public Affairs United States Government Printing Office, Washington, 2008.

Library of Congress. The Association for Diplomatic Studies and Training Foreign Affairs Oral History Project.

Konstantinos Karamanlis Archive2005. Gegonota kai Keimena [Events and texts]. *Published documents* vol. 8. Athens: Kathimerini.

Secondary sources

Athanasopoulou, E., 1999. *Tourkia. Anazitisi Asfaleias. Amerikano-Vretanika Simferonta* [*Turkey: Anglo-American Interests 1945–1952*]. Athens: Papazisis Publisher.

Attalides, M., 2003. *Cyprus. Nationalism and International Politics*. Peleus. Studien zur Archäologie und Geschichte Griechenlands und Zyperns Bd 18. Mannheim-Möhnesee: Bibliopolis.

Bahcheli, T., 1990. *Greek-Turkish Relations since 1955*. New York: Avalon Publishing.

Camp, G., 1980. Greek-Turkish conflict over Cyprus. *Political Science Quarterly*, 95 (1), 43–70.

Chourchoulis, D., & Kourkouvelas, L., 2012. Greek perceptions of NATO during the Cold War, *Southeast European and Black Sea Studies*, 12 (4), 497–514.

Couloumbis, Th., 1996. *To Kypriako Zitima. Lathi, Didagmata and Prooptikes* [*The Cyprus Question. Mistakes, Lessons and Prospects*]. Athens: Sideris.

Hatzivassiliou, E., 2006. *Greece and the Cold War. Frontline state, 1952–1967.* London and New York: Routledge.

Ignatiou, M., & Venizelos, K., 2002. *Ta Mistika archeia tou Kissinger, I apofasi gia ti Dichotomisi* [*The Secret Kissinger's Archives. The Decision for the Division of Cyprus*]. Athens: Livanis publisher.

Mallinson, W., 2016. *Kissinger and the Invasion of Cyprus: Diplomacy in the Eastern Mediterranean.* Cambridge: Cambridge Scholars Publishing.

Maragkou, K., 2009. Cold War in the Aegean Favouritism in NATO's Southeastern flank: The case of the Greek Colonels, 1967–74. *Cold War History*, 9 (3), 347–366.

Rizas, S., 2018. *Realism and Human Rights in US Policy toward Greece, Turkey, and Cyprus*: Lanham: Lexington Books.

Stergiou, A., 2022. *The Greek-Turkish Maritime Dispute. Resisting the Future.* Switzerland: Springer Nature.

Stivachtis, Y., 2010. Greek Anti-Americanism and its implications for the relations between Greece and the Hellenic diaspora in the United States. *Journal of the Greek Diaspora*, 36 (1–2), 63–98.

1 The Cyprus Crisis of 1974 revisited

The interpretation of the events that unfolded in the summer of 1974 in Cyprus has been for decades an apple of discord among scholars for national, ideological, political and other reasons. Many scholars have interpreted the entire historical period from 1954 (the raising of the Cyprus issue at the UN by Greece) to 1974 as a course followed by Britain's and the United States' machinations leading to partition. The British colonialist allegedly elevated the Turkish-Cypriot community to a disproportionally important factor on the island against the Greek-Cypriot anti-colonial struggle in the 1950s and non-alignment course in the 1960s and 1970s. On the same hermeneut trajectory, the US in collaboration with the United Kingdom nourished Turkey's aspirations in the conflict, because Turkey was an increasingly important NATO power in the south-east flank of the alliance and a potential bulwark against the Soviet Union.[1] Turkish and Turkish-Cypriot scholars predominantly perceive the Cyprus Problem primarily as the continuous attempt of Greece and the Greek-Cypriot majority to impose by force the union of Cyprus with Greece, thereby disregarding the rights of the Turkish Cypriots and violating the London–Zurich accords of 1969–1960 establishing the Republic of Cyprus. This, according to the approach, became evident in the first President of the Republic Makarios' unilateral decision to amend the constitution in 1963, leading to the intercommunal riots of 1963–1964, and in 1974 with a Greek junta instigated coup. For this reason, the Turkish intervention (the term invasion is considered an inappropriate term as it was imposed by the Greeks in international terminology) in July and August 1974 precipitating the *de facto* division of the island along ethnic lines, is labelled "Freedom Operation".

As a matter of fact, the British and Americans bear responsibility for what happened in the summer of 1974 in Cyprus. Certainly, British *divide-and-rule* policies were applied in Cyprus, especially in the 1950s,

DOI: 10.4324/9781003350033-2

as the UK was coming under increasing international pressure to give away Cyprus, and it tried to draw Ankara's attention to the "threatened rights of the Turkish minority".[2] Moreover, the UK also followed the same divisive course on the internal front in order to confront Greek-Cypriot armed revolt. It recruited almost exclusively Turkish Cypriots into the police force and encouraged the Turkish Cypriots to build their own underground movement against the Greek-Cypriot anti-colonial movement, and to cooperate with Turkey. Gradually Turkish staff officers took over the military command of the Turkish-Cypriot guerilla organisation and the then attorney in the colonial government Rauf Denktaş took over its political leadership. As expected, in 1958 intercommunal violence erupted, when the Turkish-Cypriot and Greek-Cypriot paramilitary organisations began to clash with each other and terrorise minorities in mixed villages (Drousiotis, 2006b, pp. 218–228). US responsibility should also not be denied, especially as Kissinger's actions are concerned. This study will later provide evidence of this. However, Cyprus' division seems to be the culmination of a string of developments that occurred long before the British and American machinations emerged and should not be seen as a carefully designed plan by perfidious Albion and Washington. Similarly, Turkish-Cypriot support for British colonialism had come about long before British divisive policies were applied. Furthermore, Turkey's interest in Cyprus was manifested in a forceful way before 1954 (Stefanidis, 1999, pp. 229–230; Faustmann, 2004).

Through the systematic cultivation of Greek and Turkish nationalism in the previous decades, mainly through education[3] and cultural associations, the two communities had acquired their distinct identities. Greek-Cypriot volunteers went with the blessing of the Orthodox Church, the guardian of the national ideology in Cyprus, to fight for "Mother Greece" in every conflict with the Ottoman Empire. Indeed, the nationalisation of the Greek Orthodox Church rendered nationalist ideology as an integral part of the prevailing belief system of a population that hitherto identified itself in fundamentally religious terms. Turkish Cypriots, on the contrary, developed a more secular but also distinct national identity as Turkish-speaking Muslims and perceived themselves more or less as another link in the chain of the Ottoman–Turkish national evolution. For centuries Greek- and Turkish-Cypriot children attended separate schools[4] and were influenced by the historical adversarial Greek–Turkish traditions. The educational system was used as a means to impart certain norms and values and as a cultural-educational weapon for the formation of separate national identities.[5] A part of them completed their Hellenic or Turkish education by attending universities in the two motherlands. Although Greek–Turkish animosity was not replicated in inter-communal violence, the seeds of division existed in the Cypriot society long before Greek and Turkish Cypriots developed divergent attitudes toward the British colonial yoke (Stefanidis, 1999, p. 269; Bahcheli, 1990, pp. 20–21; Persianis, 2006, pp. 41–54 and 117–150).

Cultural, educational, sports and political events and manifestations in the Cypriot society advocating union with Greece, the "Panhellenic propaganda or agitation" as the British officially labelled it, supported or encouraged by Greece occurred from the advent of the British colonialism on the island.[6] Initially, there was the illusion that the British would cede Cyprus to Greece, as had been the case with the Ionian Islands in 1864, and these activities aimed primarily to forge the bond with Greece and to acclaim the "glorious moments of the Greek nation".[7] In the course of time, however, and as it was becoming obvious that Lonon had no such intension, the demand for self-determination, meaning union with Greece, acquired a more radical form.[8] In some cases, as after the violently suppressed uprising of 1931, the British tried to contain it with aggressive measures like censorship, imprisonment and other repressive measures; however, this was, as the colonial authorities themselves admitted, without result. The "spirit of rebellion against the British rule" continued to be strong, especially among the young people who very often challenged the British rule with acts of civil disobedience.[9] Again and again, the British government complained to the Greek government for them supporting the "Panhellenic agitation on the island", instrumentalising the Greek consuls to foster "Panhellenic and anti-British Propaganda".[10]

The Turkish Cypriots also engaged in analogous activities. Turkish-Cypriot students also committed acts of disobedience against the British colonial authorities in order to honour or to conspicuously celebrate "great moments of the Ottoman and Turkish history", while Turkish consuls consistently fostered Turkish nationalism on the island, emulating the Greek consuls.[11] In the 1930s, in their reports the colonial governors noted that they were faced with a young generation of Turkish Cypriots who were Kemalists and were endeavoured to promote their own national ideals as the Greek Cypriots did.[12]

When after World War II Greek Cypriots under the leadership of the Greek orthodox Church[13] began voicing increasingly stronger and stronger their demand for union with Greece as the actualisation of their self-determination, Turkish Cypriots started reacting and to organise anti-*Enosis* gatherings and events. They not only opposed the union demand but also the self-government option out of fear of becoming subject of the administration of the numerically stronger Greek-Cypriot community.[14] They also complained with stronger intensity to the British colonial authorities about the shortage of Turkish-Cypriot teachers for the Turkish-Cypriot schools. To that purpose, they began raising funds for scholarships to enable Turkish Cypriots to study in Turkey. Organisations in Turkey also supported these fundraisings. Furthermore, the prominent personalities of the Turkish-Cypriot community did not fail to convey to the British mention that their community disliked Greek Cypriots and wished for the perpetuation of the "British administration" as a means of securing peace between the two communities.[15] According to the British, the Turkish Cypriots were, however, disorganised and their existence was seriously threatened by the absence of proper religious administration like the Greek Cypriots had. Therefore, the colonial authorities restored the office of Mufti. This was not enough to calm Turkish-Cypriot fears.[16]

Though there had been some decisions by the colonial authorities like the establishment of the *Committee for Turkish Affairs* indicating a divisive course, it appears that London did not approve of this and did not want to encourage the increase of Turkishness of the Cypriot minority as opposing the British interests in the context of the Cold War. London feared the repetition of the events in Northern Ireland and the Muslims in India.[17] In the 1930s, due to the "Italian menace", London had tried again to meet the geostrategic sensibilities of both Greece and Turkey while also bringing them closer to British strategy in the Mediterranean. As was the case with the Cold War in the 1950s, the Italian conquest of Abyssinia and Italy's megalomaniac ambition in the Mediterranean in the 1930s had rendered the understanding of Greece and Turkey imperative in the event of continued Italian hostility.[18]

Even in 1954, when the colonial *divide et impera* policies began to shape up and Ankara began getting seriously worried about the destiny of Turkish Cypriots in the event of the union of Cyprus with Greece, the British appeared to believe that the UK interests would be better served if Greek and Turkish Cypriots were to evolve into good subjects of the British Crown and not to good Greeks and Turks. Additionally, the Foreign Office made it a priority to support the Turkish government when it demonstrated a willingness to cooperate with Cyprus, provided it was treated fairly, and to continue to discourage nationalist impulses among Turks in Cyprus. Therefore, it made the suggestion to the Cyprus colonial government to make positive (if discreet) efforts to treat the Turkish government with more consideration and leniency than the Greek government, wherever its interests make it wish to take a hand in the internal affairs of Cyprus.[19] As already mentioned, this policy radically changed during the 1955–1959 Greek-Cypriot independence war entailing a deep rift between the two communities.

The treaties signed in 1959–1960 London and Zurich with the aim of settling the war, supposedly tried to accommodate the different wishes of all stakeholders in the conflict and to address the chasm between the two communities. At the same time, two additional treaties were signed which actually limited the independence of the new Republic: a) the *Treaty of Guarantee* between Cyprus, Turkey, Greece and United Kingdom providing the right to the three external powers for joint or unilateral action for re-establishing the state of constitutional order created by the London–Zurich Agreements; b) the *Treaty of Alliance* between Cyprus, Greece and Turkey providing that Greece and Turkey could station contingents of their forces in Cyprus. Apart from the fact that these two treaties gave to foreign powers the right to intervene, were never ratified by the House of Representatives of the Republic of Cyprus depriving them of democratic legitimacy (Hatzivassiliou, 2002, pp. 73–92).

The institutional structure of the new state was marked by further, fatal institutional malfeasances and inconsistencies. The constitution had a complex and dysfunctional structure. It was tailored to balance power between the Greek- and Turkish-Cypriot communities in a way that would prevent the numerically much smaller Turkish-Cypriot population from being side-lined by Greek Cypriots. Its provisions, however, celebrated the institutionalisation of ethnicity and, instead of encouraging co-operation between the ethnic communities, boosted separatist tendencies via the creation of separate municipalities, separate communal chambers and separate electoral rolls. Influenced by the very spirit of its constitution, the public life of Cyprus leaned, therefore, towards ethnic antagonism instead of a real democratic practice and the growth of class-based party politics. Although the treaties forbade activities promoting the ineffable desire for partition and union with the motherlands Greece and Turkey, they were designed to ensure that political rights derived from communal allegiance rather the state allegiance overdetermining the destiny of the new state and causing permanent tensions between the two communities. Large parts of the Greek-Cypriot community and their leadership considered the status of independence as treason to the ideal of

Enosis for which they had fought during the anti-colonial war during 1955–1959. Turkish Cypriots, on the contrary, were content with the settlements for the same reasons Greek Cypriots were not: it guaranteed Turkey's strategic control over the island via the Turkish Cypriots, the right to maintain Turkish troops on the island and to intervene, even unilaterally, in the case of violations of the treaties. The status of the Turkish-Cypriot minority had been upgraded to a political almost equal and in some respects even privileged community due to the veto rights their representatives retained. For some Turkish Cypriots, this settlement was even more favourable than partition, since they did not have to leave their homes and properties (Faustmann, 2004, p. 212; Markides, 2002, pp. 51–52.).

Nevertheless, there also were hardliners in the Turkish-Cypriot community, mainly around the State Attorney in the British colonial era, Rauf Denktash, who regarded the establishment of the Republic of Cyprus in 1960 with a clear majority of the Greek-Cypriot community as something equal to union with Greece that could not be tolerated by Turkey for long time (Soulioti, 2006, pp. 135–146; Richter, 2007, pp. 161–188).

In January 1963, the disagreement on the issue of the separate municipalities was added to the long chain of unsuccessful efforts to implement the constitution of the new state. Since repeated attempts to solve the disputes failed, President Makarios decided to act unilaterally in November 1963 and to submit to the three guarantor powers proposals with 13 constitutional amendments, containing among other things the abolition of the veto power by both the President and the Vice-President, and aiming, in his view, at allowing a better functioning of the government. Turkey and Turkish Cypriots perceived this move as a blatant provocation. In December 1963, bicommunal clashes erupted, which immediately spilled over to Greece and Turkey bringing the two allies to the verge of war that was averted by a US intervention. The Turkish Cypriots resigned from their posts in the state and retreated into armed enclaves, because they feared for their safety, although Makarios immediately called for their return. Eventually, it was the United Nations that managed to bring about peace on the island, by dispatching a permanent, as it has since been shown, UN peacekeeping force to Cyprus in response to Security Council Resolution 186 of 1964. The political climate on the island remained, however, toxic and polarised (Ker-Lindsay, 2004).

The *Treaty of Alliance* permitted Greece and Turkey to station a force of 950 (ELDYK) and 650 (TOURDYK) men respectively on the island. After the intercommunal riots in 1963/1964, the Cyprus government decided in February 1964 to build up the so-called National Guard, which was mainly Greek-officered. With Turkey's support, the Turkish Cypriots also built up their own separate paramilitary army that shaped up from 1971 onwards into a regular and well-organised army. Both troops drew their members from the regular draft. In 1973, the Turkish-Cypriot army began to hire some former conscripts on the basis of three- or five-years contracts. Both armies clandestinely brought weapons to the island from various countries.[20]

Things were aggravated by the takeover of power by some military colonels in Greece in April 1967.[21] The latter believed they could easily realise the "vision" of union with Greece, even elicit Turkey's consent to this by granting them a base in return, as previous plans for the settlement of the Cyprus Issue had provided for. A still disputed bloody incident at the Turkish-Cypriot enclave at Kofinou and Agios Theodoros between the National Guard of Cyprus and the Turkish-Cypriot paramilitaries in 1967 worsened the rift between the communities. Upon Ankara's threat to invade Cyprus, Athens was compelled to withdraw the Greek division, stationed at that time in Cyprus, back to Greece. On the island remained some Greek officers, leading members of the National Guard, who gradually formed a pro-*Enosis* group called the *National Front* heavily opposed to the Archbishop and President of the Republic Cyprus Makarios. In a bid to calm down tempers, Greece and Turkey agreed to initiate talks on a new constitutional structure of Cyprus which never came to any conclusion (Rizas, 2002/2003, pp. 240–242).

Makarios' controversial action to reject the Turkish-Cypriot demand for more local autonomy in return for relinquishing the privileges granted to the Turkish-Cypriot community by the Zurich Agreements out of fear that this would undermine the unitary character of the state, further soured his tensed relations with the Turkish Cypriots. He also tolerated the existence of the enclaves, where about 20% of the Turkish-Cypriot population was confined between 1963 and 1974, being excluded from the prosperity which Cyprus enjoyed at the same time (Göktepe, 2005, pp. 431–432).

His most embittered enemies were the colonels in Athens who were furious by Makarios' noncompliance with their political preferences, as Makarios began building ties with the Soviet Bloc demonstrating his intention to follow a completely different foreign policy course than Athens and Ankara that had joined NATO decades ago (Stergiou, 2021, p. 79).

More precisely, during the military junta (1967–1974), the partisan sentiments within the Greek-Cypriot community between the pro-union forces and Makarios, backed at the time by the powerful Cypriot Communist party, increased more and more, especially since the former leader of the anti-colonial struggle, Georgios Grivas, returned to Cyprus in August 1971 and formed an underground armed organisation, the so-called EOKA B. EOKA B's main aspiration was to force Makarios to change his policy and adopt a pro-union course with Greece. In Grivas followers' eyes, Makarios was simply a traitor to the ideal of *Enosis*. Furthermore, Grivas seems to have enjoyed support from the most hardline wing of the military regime in Athens. Despite Makarios' electoral success, Grivas supporters launched a full-fledged terrorist activity against him and his supporters that led to a vicious circle of violence and anti-violence amounting to a low-scale civil war from 1971 to 1974 within the Greek-Cypriot community. Both pro-Makarios and anti-Makarios forces put armed paramilitary groups together and started fighting heavily with each other even within the Cypriot Orthodox Church institution. In February 1972, the government averted at the very last moment a coup d'état and an assassination attempt. Following the failed assassination against him, Makarios decided to purge the police and his presidential guard of non-loyal members, which was perceived by the Greek pro-junta officers on the island as a bitter provocation, because the recruits were assumed Communists.[22]

The vision of *Enosis*, however, as even the Greek militaries in Cyprus admitted,[23] changed in the course of time and started being perceived differently by Greek Cypriots in Cyprus and Greeks in the motherland Greece. While in Greece, the pro-union forces imagined it as a full institutional incorporation of Cyprus into the Greek state, many Cypriots, especially those occupying significant posts in the Cyprus Republic imagined it rather as a cultural, psychological, national union with Greece. A big part of the Cypriot society was, according to the Greek militaries' reports, negatively disposed towards the Greek officers servicing in the National Guard as well as Greece in general. This anti-Hellenic culture was, according to them, nurtured by the Cypriot Communist party and the Makarios government.[24]

The intercommunal talks aimed at solving the problems that emerged out of the bicommunal clashes in 1963–1964 did not make appreciable progress, as Greek–Turkish relations were soured once again a few years later, despite efforts to show to the allies a conciliatory attitude. The military regime in Athens was convinced that the disrupting element in the Greek–Turkish rapprochement was the Archbishop and President of the Republic of Cyprus Makarios who "would be inclined to reject anything proposed by Greece or Turkey".

On the other side, Makarios preferred the mediation of the United Nations which he saw as refuge from Athens and Ankara.[25]

At the same time, the Greece-Turkey relationship deteriorated as well. Athens was also complaining about Turkish training flights in the Aegean, which in their opinion penetrated deeply into Greek airspace, came within a few miles of the Greek capital and were not conducted in accordance with ICAO (International Civil Aviation Organisation) regulations. The Greek air force was placed in an Orange state, a NATO alert condition indicating possible enemy attack within hours. Athens' estimation was that these actions were part of a concerted Turkish attack including a Turkish press campaign against the Muslim, Turkish-speaking minority in Greek Thrace and an increasingly hardened Turkish position on the Cyprus question. Ankara, on the other hand, claimed that the flights over the Aegean were training exercises and they were conducted according to NATO regulations that were similar to ICAO regulations. Therefore, they argued, those exercises had to take place over the Aegean, since, under NATO regulations, such flights could no longer be operated over the Black Sea. They also claimed that Greeks were trying to turn the Aegean into a "sort of *mare nostrum*". In November 1967, the US embassies in Ankara and Athens were instructed to dampen the tensions between the two countries.[26]

In his watching brief on the Greek–Turkish relations and Cyprus of November 1970 and November 1971. NATO's Secretary General admitted that the hopes for a settlement based on the negotiations between the two communities may well be regarded as weaker now than some time ago despite the good relations between Athens and Ankara. Thus, it was to be feared that if the situation on the island itself continued indefinitely, relations between Greece and Turkey could be affected and reverse "the encouraging improvement which was witnessed in the last two years". Such a possible future development would be particularly regrettable, if viewed against the background of the general situation in the Mediterranean.[27]

In January 1974, Grivas died and the control of his EOKA B organisation was taken over directly by Athens. After the announcement of Grivas' death, Archbishop Makarios granted full amnesty to all the wanted members of EOKA B and released all prisoners from the prisons as a gesture of goodwill and an end to the confrontation. On the contrary, EOKA B issued an order on 6 February 1974 with guidelines for its re-organisation with a view to continuing its terrorist activities. Makarios's decision, however, to transfer some Greek officers and to reduce the mandatory military service from 24 to 12 months in the summer of 1974 were regarded by the Greek junta-led officers as s blatant provocation and as proof of Makarios' treasonous behaviour. In a letter to the "President of the Hellenic Republic" Faidon Gkizikis, Makarios tried to justify his decision and placate the military regime that he was not wishing to sever ties with Greece but to foster a relationship on the basis of the existence of two equal and independent states (Hellenic Parliament and House of Representatives, 2018, pp. 62–65 and 330).

This state of affairs, however, meant the loss of military and political control of Cyprus by Greece as well as the humiliation of Dimitrios Ioannides, the new radical Head of the Greek junta. In June and July 1974, Ioannidis, a hardliner and by all accounts a reckless dilettante in foreign policy, communicated to the Americans his conflicting and unclear plans to overthrow Makarios. The US response was equally vague and unclear. On the one hand, Ioannides got the message not to attempt a union of Cyprus, on the other hand, he never got an unambiguous message to halt action against Archbishop Makarios (Rizas, 2002/2003, pp. 247–248).

Eventually, it was Ioannides, who, decided to implement his plan, who ordered and coordinated, in collaboration with Brigadier A. Kondylis, in July 1974 the overthrow of Archbishop and President Makarios and his replacement by a puppet regime consisting of people known for their strong anti-Turkish-Cypriot feelings. In one *WikiLeaks* CIA report of 16 July 1979, about possible leak of CIA memoranda on 1974 Cyprus Crisis, also published in the newspaper *To Vima* at the time, the dictator Ioannides is said to have claimed that the United States encouraged him to go ahead with the coup attempt, rather than attempting to persuade him to change his mind. Therefore, Turkey's invasion to Cyprus came as a surprise, making him believe that he had been betrayed by the Americans. The documents allegedly show that the CIA had clear information about the coup in Cyprus (which was, however, systematically underestimated by the US embassy in Athens) as well as Turkish invasion plans. We do not know who leaked the document but the CIA agent who authored the report, reveals little to sustain the allegations of the "role of the Americans" in the 1974 Cyprus Crisis.[28]

US Ambassador in Athens Tasca's appraisal of the political situation in Greece and Cyprus in July 1974, is, however, more ambiguous. In his report to the State Department on 14 July 1974, Tasca estimated that, regarding Cyprus, Ioannides saw one of two things happening: either Cyprus would slowly drift left and become a Cuba of the Mediterranean (this drift would be caused by the communist propaganda, which was being taught in the school system), or the 80% Greek majority would achieve union with Greece. The one thing that could not happen, was union with Turkey. Regarding Greece, Tasca assessed that Greece really did not want war with Turkey concluding that the only winner in such a war would be the Soviet Union. Greece would not attack Turkey pre-emptively but would not permit Greek interests in the Aegean (Aegean oil rights) or Cyprus to be jeopardised. The United States could assist in preventing a Greek–Turkish war by selling Greece the arms it needed to achieve a level of military strength sufficient to prevent a successful Turkish attack on Greece.[29]

In any case, the conspirators' plan was to capture the Presidential Palace in Nicosia and arrest or perhaps assassinate Makarios. However, the plan succeeded only partially. The presidential palace was almost entirely burned down but Makarios narrowly escaped death by fleeing the building from its back door. From there he managed to reach Paphos, a stronghold of his supporters in the south-west of the island, and to ask the British government for help. Thanks to their help, he flew from the British Military Base in Akrotiri to Malta and from there to London. On 19 July, he attended a United Nations Security Council meeting in New York at which he made his famous, but still contentious, speech, in which he stated that Cyprus was invaded by Greece, calling on Turkey to help. Meanwhile, the puppet regime at home proclaimed the establishment of the *Hellenic Republic of Cyprus*. Since the Turkish government thought that the *Treaty of Guarantee* bestowed it the right to look for ways to prevent the entrenchment of a situation that could lead to the union of Cyprus with Greece, it decided to invade Cyprus on 20 July 1974. On 23 July, finding themselves under enormous pressure, both the dictatorship in Athens and the puppet regime in Nicosia appointed by the colonels collapsed and two new governments under the old, experienced and very competent politician, Konstantinos Karamanlis in Athens, and Glafkos Klerides in Nicosia took over. Karamanlis's coalition government priority after the collapse of the junta was to elicit the support of the majority of Greeks and to "rally them around the flag". The recognition of the Greek Communist Party served that aim, since it addressed the general shift to the left which was conspicuous in the public feeling. On the same trajectory, Karamanlis paved the way for the punishment of the leaders of the two military coups (1967 and 1973),[30] released all the political prisoners and those who were interned under the military regime as well as restored to their positions those sacked during the junta (Kaminis, 2014, pp. 499–502).

On 25 July, formal peace talks began in Geneva between Greece, Turkey and the UK. In mid-August 1974, and while another round of discussions was being held in Geneva, Turkey surprisingly resumed its offensive, this time extending its occupation over about 37% of the island to what became known as the *Attila Line*. Two days later, the UN Security Council recorded "its formal disapproval of the uni- lateral military actions undertaken against the Republic of Cyprus" (Richter, 2009, pp. 378–514). Before developments reached this point, a string of tragi-comic events took place.

To this day, there is a commonly-held position in Turkey that the Turkish invasion was a "peace operation" stemming from Turkey's guarantor power obligations, carried out with a view to restore the status quo ante in the Republic of Cyprus and protect the Turkish-Cypriot minority from the Greek-Cypriot menace and the prosecu- tions of the puppet regime (Bozarslan, 2004, p. 84). It also has been argued that Turkey's intervention was well-timed and necessary because there was a possibility that both the US and the UK could recognise the new regime in Cyprus. Thus, in order to completely eliminate the Greek Cypriot's military and economic suppressions, and to prevent the unification of the island with Greece, the Turkish government had to militarily intervene (Işıksal, 2015, p. 303).

Therefore, the situation after the ceasefire of 23 July was not regar- ded as a successful end of the operation. By occupying Kyrenia, Turkish forces had gained a foothold and secured access to the sea for the Nicosia Turkish-Cypriot enclave. The majority of the Turkish-Cypriot enclaves and hence of the Turkish-Cypriot population was, however, outside of the Turkish army-controlled area. The Turkish troops were in vary bad shape, since the logistical line had collapsed. While the Geneva conference was being held, Turkey transported more troops and ammunition to the island bracing for the second stage of the invasion. It is obvious that the Turkish side had no intention at all to return to the status quo ante that in Turkish eyes had enabled the Greek Cypriots to discriminate against and to threaten the security of Turkish Cypriots (Bahcheli, 1990 pp. 98–100).

According to the 1959 and 1960 London–Zurich Agreements, how- ever, the commitment of the guarantor powers should be construed as limited only to the restoration of the constitutional order. Therefore, the Security Council in its resolution 353(1974) called upon all states *to respect the sovereignty, independence and territorial integrity of Cyprus; and demanded an immediate end to foreign military interven- tion in Cyprus that was in contravention of its sovereignty, independence and territorial integrity; requested the withdrawal without delay from the Republic of Cyprus of foreign military personnel present otherwise than under the authority of international agreements, including those whose withdrawal was requested by the President of the Republic of Cyprus, Archbishop Makarios, on 2 July 1974* (United Nations Department of Public Information, 1974, p. 265).

Against this background, it should not escape our attention that Turkey had repeatedly declared officially it would respond by force any attempt aimed at realising union with Greece. This was obvious in August 1964, when Turkey sent its air force against the Greek Cypriots and in November 1967 by demanding the withdrawal of the Greek troops from the island. According to some Turkish scholars (Bahcheli, 1989, pp. 87–88) the Greek-Cypriot leadership had never renounced the *Enosis* ideology and was not ready to surrender local autonomy to the Turkish Cypriots in the bicommunal talks from 1968–1974.

Other Turkish scholars have not failed to point out that on 30 July 1974 in Geneva almost all Turkish demands were satisfied, mainly the recognition of local autonomy for the Turkish-Cypriot community. The Turkish generals, however, were pushing for permission to continue the military operation warning that, under the current circumstances, the Turkish army was strategically not in a position to repel a counter-offensive. Therefore, during the Geneva talks, the hardliner leader of the Turkish Community, Rauf Denktash, went a step further and demanded not only the recognition of local autonomy but the establishment of a federal state, which could not be accepted by the Greek mission (Firat, 2012, pp. 179–186).

All in all, while there is a legal basis for the first Turkish invasion as a response to the Greece-instigated military coup as a means to enforce the status quo ante, there is no legal basis at all, as independent scholars also pointed out, for the second stage of the Turkish invasion and of course of the prolonged stay of Turkish troops in Cyprus ever since (Ker-Lindsay, 2011, p. 45).

NATO's reaction to these stormy developments is a hallmark of the inert and highly bureaucratic nature of the organisation at the time, confirming that NATO is a rather ponderous organisation, whose decision-making relies on the unanimity principle and thus susceptible to disputes that can paralyse it (Hatzivassiliou, 2020, p. 102).

The Military Committee of the alliance met on 22 July for the first time in order to assess the situation in Cyprus and in the Greek–Turkish relations. On 23 July amidst intelligence on the movements of three Bulgarian divisions close to the Greek/Turkish frontier, the Military Committee met again but again without being able to complete a full assessment. Amid a waging war, NATO decided to task its bodies to conduct a wider review of recent events in Cyprus and how these events affected the alliance as a whole. The study should be based on factual reports about the movement of the forces retained under Greek and Turkish national control. Only then it would be possible to produce an assessment not based "on uncertain and unsubstantiated evidence", because NATO had so far received only two messages from the Turkish General Staff.

Greece's representative in the committee, Lieutenant General J. Korkas, reported to the chairman of the committee, both orally and in writing, the continued fighting in Cyprus but the Chairman did not proceed into any action except to convey the information to the Secretary General – who had already received the information through official channels but he was on holidays during the crucial time – suggesting that these were not matters on which the Military Committee could act. He was supported on this by the UK representative, whose position was of paramount importance given the UK's role as Guarantor Power of the Cyprus Republic. Apparently, the United Kingdom's concern was about the operation of the British Military Bases and the British sea forces, around Cyprus which conducted security evacuations of British civilians and others who were in danger from clashes on the island. He also relinquished any responsibility of the Committee, underplayed the events and procrastinated the making of a decision, underscoring the difficulties of making a proper assessment without full inputs from all nations concerned. The UK's suggestion was to follow the same procedure NATO had followed in the Autumn of 1973, when a situation, albeit far less grave, occurred in Iceland. Ultimately, the paper was sent to the Council and served a useful purpose and this also was required for Cyprus. Against this background, the Committee's only action was to establish an *Open-Ended Ad Hoc Working Group* to study the broad military implications to NATO from the Cyprus Crisis.[31]

To this respect, the French delegation prepared a memorandum for the members of the Military Committee on how the *Cyprus Working Group*, which was supposed to meet on 26 July 1974, should deal with the situation. The French proposal was that the *Cyprus Working Group* should consider the background paper that had been submitted on 22 July with a view to completing a skeleton paper so that the staff would subsequently produce a first outline working paper for consideration at the following meeting of the Working Group.[32]

Against the backdrop of the breakdown of the Geneva talks and Greece's decision to withdraw its forces from the integrated structure of

NATO,[33] the Military Committee of the alliance met again on 14 August 1974. In a different climate, most of the members voiced their concern over the actions on Cyprus and their hopes that Greece would reconsider its decision to leave NATO as Athens had announced in order to protest NATO's reluctance to take action against Turkey. The Committee then considered what actions would be appropriate ahead of the withdrawal of Greek forces from NATO. Since the study still stood out, it was proposed to prepare a preliminary review, in close co-ordination with SHAPE, that would serve as a basis for a more comprehensive study as events unfurled, and would provide the foundation for a detailed assessment![34]

Obviously, the alliance members were either reluctant to engage in any action in Cyprus or completely indifferent to what was unfolding on the island. As a matter of fact, NATO was not empowered to act beyond its accepted remit and against an alliance member like Turkey to protect a non-alliance member like Cyprus which happened also to be a member of the relatively anti-Western Non-Aligned Movement. However, the alliance appeared to neglect the importance of Cyprus for its cohesion in this sensitive region underscored by all Secretary Generals since 1964. As it has been aptly mentioned, it was the first time in post-war European history that a NATO member, using NATO weapons, took 35,000 of its forces out of the NATO structure in order to occupy part of another democratic European country and member of the western community (Moustakis, 2003, p. 32).

Furthermore, in his watching briefs of 1972 and 1973, General Secretary Joseph Lunz had pointed out that Cyprus, because of its highly positive implications for the Southern flank of the alliance, constituted a precious affirmation of the allied will for solidarity in the sector of the eastern Mediterranean where the situation continues to give cause for concern.[35]

Therefore, Athens blamed NATO officials for pushing Greece to withdraw from the military structure of NATO due to the alliance's reluctance to avert the aggression of a member-state against an independent state member of the United Nations as well as their inability or unwillingness to intervene to prevent the Turkish attack or to proceed into a decisive action. Greece's request for the immediate convening of the NATO Council, for example, was rejected on the ground that this was impossible at that time due to the absence of the Council members on summer holidays: In the Greek withdrawal statement, it was mentioned that ... *the Alliance Treaty could not and was not intended to encourage aggression by its signatories either against non-member countries or against each other ... However, recent events in Cyprus have revealed grave weaknesses in the fabric of the alliance.*

Fundamental provisions of the Treaty regulating relations among member countries and obligating them to use peaceful manner for the composition of their differences were disregarded ... Arms provided to be used in the common defence of the alliance were turned against an independent member-state of the United Nations, to sow death and destruction and ultimately to lead to its dismemberment ... Using naked force, Turkey violated all the relevant resolutions of the Security Council and all the ceasefire agreements, in utter and cynical contempt of all norms of international order and morality. It is now evident that the aim of the massive Turkish forces which landed on Cyprus in violation of existing treaties was not to protect the island's Turkish minority but to implement Turkey's expansionist and imperialist plans ... Faced with these tragic events, when a member of the alliance attacked an independent country, the alliance reacted with surprising apathy, strangely limiting itself to the role of a mere bystander ... Under these circumstances Greece, as Athens argued, was forced to draw the necessary conclusions. If the alliance was not in a position to prevent an armed conflict between two of its members, would it be able to come to their support in the event of a danger from outside? Greece had therefore decided to assume itself the protection of the independence of Greece and place again the Greek land, sea, and air forces heretofore assigned to the integrated allied military organisation under national command.[36]

On the same trajectory, on 25 September 1974, in his farewell speech to his NATO colleagues, the permanent Greek representative to NATO, Ambassador A. Chorafas, accused the alliance members of hypocrisy. According to Chorafas, some people in Greece were wondering whether their allies' hostility during "the past seven years" (sic during the military junta) was, in fact, directed against the colonels' regime or whether it could be ascribed to other factors; whether the allied governments were genuinely interested in a change of the regime or whether their apparent interest was only a facade designed as a sop for public opinion; and, lastly, whether they have any real intention of helping the new Athenian democracy, frail and unsteady as it still was, to grow in strength and develop its potentialities to the full. When put to the test in the Cyprus Crisis, the alliance was found wanting, and even powerless.[37]

In his report on his watching brief to the ministerial meeting of NATO in December 1974, Joseph Luns tried to entertain the bad impression of NATO's inertia during the summer crisis by asserting that the Cyprus Crisis came as a complete surprise and thus the only possible form of action by then was to try as a matter of urgency to contain its effects and to find a speedy solution. The measures he took, so Luns continued, were directed to this end and operated at two levels: at the level of intensive consultations in the Council that made repeated appeals for restraint while, at the same time, supporting the efforts to find a peaceful solution made under United Kingdom auspices; at the level of his personal action realm, within which he sent several urgent messages to the Ankara and Athens governments appealing to them to defuse the confrontation and offering mediation by visiting the two capitals. However, even Luns admitted that it was hard to reconcile these developments with the principles of co-operation solemnly reaffirmed in the NATO Ottawa Declaration, which had been signed barely a month before.[38]

In reality, Luns' intervention was limited to a few approaches to the Turkish and Greek permanent representatives to NATO on the explosive situation looming in their bilateral relations in Spring and June 1974 and only after having been contacted by the US permanent representative to NATO to urge moderation before the tense state of Greek/Turkish relations fully derailed. However, he contended himself with the assurances of the two governments that "they would act in a low key over the issues involved".[39]

The US embassy noticed in August 1974 that the government of Greece and the Greek people were highly frustrated because of their inability to come to the aid of their fellow Greeks in Cyprus. The conflict with Turkey was aggravated by the fact that its historic adversary Turkey was involved. During the crisis, Greece felt let down by its NATO allies which it felt could have compelled Turkey to uphold the ceasefire. However, it was believed that, when the dust settled, the basic elements tying Greece to the United States and its NATO allies would be given their appropriate weight ... *they are a small country surrounded by hostile and potentially hostile forces. geographically, they clearly need friends* ...[40]

Nevertheless, the view, that there had been a NATO plan to divide the island between the NATO members Greece and Turkey in order to transform the island to a NATO basis (Kadritzke & Wagner, 1976) is rather a conspiracy theory. Brendan O'Malley and Ian Craig went so far as to argue that the Cyprus Crisis was no failure of American diplomacy, but a deliberate Cold War plot to divide the island and save the top-secret spying and defence facilities from the twin threats of a communist takeover or British withdrawal. The plot was allegedly devised by the US in order to prevent Makarios from turning Cyprus into a Soviet satellite (O'Malley & Craig, 2001).

Although there is no doubt that Turkey had been more important for the alliance than Greece, in reality, NATO's strategy was reactive rather than proactive. The historical experience is a hallmark of this. In the following decades, the occupied territory was never used by NATO. On the contrary, the prolongation of the Cyprus Problem has been a permanent headache for the alliance (Asmussen, 2008, pp. 89–90; Drousiotis, 2014, p. 582).

It is not clear enough whether the US foreign policy at that time impacted NATO's course to the crisis. According to newly revealed declassified information, Henry Kissinger, US Secretary of State at the time, seems to have backed the Turkish invasion. Kissinger is supposed to have told then-US President Gerald Ford that Turkey was entitled to seize part of the island, confirming what several historians and journalists have asserted about the US Secretary of State's involvement in the Cypriot affairs in 1974. A day before the second invasion wave of Turkish forces in Cyprus in 1974, Secretary of State Henry Kissinger told President Gerald Ford – in office only four days after Richard Nixon resigned, facing impeachment over Watergate – that if Greece went to war with Turkey that America should back the Turks and that they were entitled to seize part of the island.[41]

In support of this and contrary to some authors' claim that Cyprus' strategic location due to the communications and the Sovereign Base Areas did not merit the importance attached to them by the "conspiracy theorists", William Mallinson and Vassilis Fouskas have provided significant documentary evidence that Kissinger quite clearly did not see Cyprus as a priority. Therefore, he questioned Britain's wish to apply pressure on the Greek junta to withdraw their officers from Cyprus, speciously using communism as an excuse to delay supporting international law. Kissinger also refused to support any decisive action over Cyprus illogically stating that pressure to restore Makarios would strengthen the Athens junta. More importantly for this study, he did not wish to face a NATO ministerial meeting while Turkey was attacking with a view to achieving a *fait accompli* with a relative impunity (Mallinson & Fouskas, 2017).

William Mallinson in his well-known book about Kissinger also maintains that on 20 July, Kissinger instructed Tasca to inform the Greek government that if it attacked Turkey and announced union with Greece, the US would immediately cut off military aid, while, simultaneously, he fought hard against Congress' decision to suspend the supply of American arms to Turkey. Furthermore, his unwillingness to delegate had lowered the morale and effectiveness of the Department of State and had made American diplomacy lop-sided. Kissinger seemed to be clearly suspicious that if Makarios returned to power in those circumstances, would not hesitate to regard the

Russians as his saviours and allow an already strong communist party to gain further strength (Mallinson, 2016, pp. 83–120).

The well-known Greek Journalist Alexis Papachelas in his investigative book on the Greek military junta, points out Kissinger's obsession with geopolitical *realpolitik*, always in favour of US interests, with the Watergate scandal looming in the background, also underscoring Kissinger's overt cynicism. This is the case when he reproaches Tasca saying that *... we are the State Department, not a university department of political sciences ...* or when he confidentially informs former US president Glenn Ford that *... there is no American reason for the Turks to not hold a third of Cyprus ...* Papachelas also pinpoints Kissinger's friendly attitude towards Turkey and his fellow Harvard alumnus Bulent Ecevit (Papachelas, 2021, pp. 210–211 and 527–528).

The US Congress also savaged Kissinger for his actions. Many Congress members even demanded to be ousted from his position, as there was a great concern about the consequences his policy could have on US military presence in Greece.[42]

Kissinger in his turn tried to stall and hinder US Congress' decision to impose an arms embargo on Turkey[43] in many ways, most notably by refusing to make public domain the memorandum of the Legal Service of the State Department on the Turkish invasion of Cyprus. According to the memorandum, Turkey had used in Cyprus US weapons not for defence purposes as provided by the delivery agreement but for aggression ones (Theodorakopoulos, 1996, pp. 108–116).

Another well-known, investigative journalist, Christopher Hitchens, in his famous book, *The Trial of Henry Kissinger*, claims that Kissinger *did have advance knowledge of the plan to depose and kill Makarios ...* Hitchens substantiates his assertion with a memorandum Kissinger evidently received from the head of his State Department Cyprus desk, Thomas Boyatt, in which the latter argued that *... in the absence of a US demarche to Athens, warning the dictators to desist, it might be assumed that the United States was indifferent to this. And he added what everybody knew – that such a coup, if it went forward, would beyond doubt trigger a Turkish invasion ...* (Hitchens, 2001, p. 60).

Other scholars, however, have been sceptical about the criticism against Kissinger and the USA in general. So, it has been argued that President Ford's handling of relations with Greece was focused on crisis management rather than crisis solving. Ford and his Secretary of State Henry Kissinger, developed the concept of a "balanced approach" towards Athens and Ankara in political, economic and military terms that aimed at ensuring close ties with both. It is Carter's and policy concept's merit, that Greece attained a return to full

NATO membership despite Turkish resistance. The "misunderstanding" about Kissinger's policy should be attributed to the fact that many of his actions towards Turkey were kept secret (Antonopoulos, 2016).

In February 1978, during a parliamentary discussion on the US military bases in Greece, the Greek Defence Minister Evangelos Averof was challenged to comment on the accusations against the United States about their role during the Turkish invasion of Cyprus. The US allegedly impeded movements of Greek troops and supplies to the island, interfered with Greek radars, gave unspecified "information" to the Turks, forced Greek ships to return by employing American aircraft from the US military base in Souda (Crete), and used "threats" to turn back Greek air force planes. Averof labelled these claims "exaggerated rumours" and declared that his careful study of the matter had convinced him that such interventions had not been proven anywhere and that he had seen no evidence from US or Greek sources to support these claims. He acknowledged, however, that the allies did attempt diplomatic interventions but that these were unsuccessful.[44] Although Averof was well-disposed towards the Americans, his witness should be taken seriously into consideration, because he had every reason to embrace this approach to the events. Averof participated in Konstantinos Karamanlis's government that took over from the colonels and took the final decision for withdrawal of the Greek army and hence has ever since been blasted for defeatism and not doing enough to help Cyprus. This explanation would provide a convenient alibi.

As a matter of fact, in early June 1974, Kissinger was informed by the British about the Athens military regime's foreign policy antics. At the same time, he was also encouraged by senior official agents of the State Department to step in and to convey to the Greek regime private signals of American anxiety. Kissinger, however, was reluctant to do that and to see the United States involved in the Greek–Turkish dispute, as "he believed firmly that any change for the better must be left for the Greeks to bring about themselves". He also had the strong opinion that "public displays of indignation against the military regime did not help".[45]

It seems that Kissinger's exclusive concern and apparently the only motive for his actions was a possible Soviet penetration into Cyprus and in the eastern Mediterranean. Kissinger's fears about Soviet penetration into the island, however, were exaggerated. As we have shown elsewhere, Moscow was remarkably self-restrained during the Cyprus Crisis. Kremlin's strategic interests in the region did not dovetail with the survival of Makarios, as President of the Republic.

Non-accidentally, the Kremlin avoided exercising any pressure, or even issuing the faintest warning against the impending Turkish military intervention, although it was registered by the Soviet satellites. Turkey was simply more important for the Soviets than Cyprus and Greece (Stergiou, 2021, pp. 80–83). Today, we also know from declassified NATO documents that NATO intelligence did not identify any unusual alert measures by the Soviets or other Warsaw Pact nations at the crucial time.[46]

In the top-secret study of the General Staff of the National Guard on the situation in Cyprus in May 1974 it was speculated that the US embassy had come to terms with Makarios' policy believing that the Church of Cyprus could contain communism in the Cypriot society and engaged in cultural and economic activities for that purpose. The Soviets, on the contrary, backed by the other countries of the Eastern Bloc were providing general support to the Cypriot Communists and were actively involved in the Cypriot politics and social activities.[47]

In the recount of the events in Cyprus that Admiral Petros Arapakis submitted to Karamanlis after the restoration of democracy in Greece, it is mentioned that the Greek dictator Ioannides was surprised by the Turkish response and enraged at the Americans claiming that they had deceived him. He believed that Turkey was also content with the ouster of Makarios and could come to a compromise with Greece at some stage in the future not only for Cyprus but probably also to set up a joint company for the discovery of oil deposits in the Aegean and share the profits from its exploitation. When he realised that things did not unfold differently as planned, he tried to blackmail the Americans by threatening to withdraw from NATO. Nevertheless, these tactics did not work out.[48]

The US denial to deliver in August 1974 the F4 air fighters to Greece that had been ordered a long time ago, caused additional anger in Athens. Only upon Athens' blackmail that it had the intention to conclude a military deal with France, earmarking the purchase of Mirage air fighters instead of the US aeroplanes, did Kissinger bother to send a message to Ecevit to stop the deployment of the Turkish troops in Cyprus. It was too late (Papachelas, 2021, pp. 529–539).

US inactivity is astonishing given that a short time before the events, the US mission to NATO had warned about the deteriorating situation in Greek–Turkish relations, suggesting an urgent review of the US policy towards Greece. On the same trajectory, the US Ambassadors in Greece and Turkey suggested that both the US Secretary General and SACEUR should take immediately informal initiatives "outside of the formal NATO framework".[49]

The role of the British is another non-adequately elucidated aspect of the eventful summer of 1974. After the Turkish invasion, the British government quickly made it clear that it was not willing to exercise the right of intervention as formulated in the Treaty of Guarantee, article IV stating that in the event of a breach of the provisions of the Treaty ... *each of the three guarantor powers reserves the right to take action with the sole aim of re-establishing the state of affairs created by the present Treaty* ... The UK interpreted, however, its obligation very loosely or very strictly. According to the UK official view, the Guarantee Treaty gives the signatory parties the legal right but does not obligate them to intervene in support of the Zurich Agreements (Tsardanidis, 1988, p. 117).

Although the United Kingdom did never seriously consider an intervention, that would embroil the British Sovereign Bases on Cyprus into the conflict, it tried diplomatically to discourage Turkey from doing anything that could lead to war with Greece and hence to endanger NATO's south-eastern flank. Furthermore, after the violent ouster of President Makarios, the British Foreign Minister James Callaghan informed Kissinger of the British position, which coincided with that of the European Economic Community, namely, that the ideal solution would be the return of Makarios. Kissinger, however, was reluctant to accept Makarios back and to commit him as President of Cyprus (Asmussen, 2008, pp. 56–59).

Documents from the National Archives of Australia showed that Britain did not object the occupation by Turkish military forces of about one-third of the island before agreeing to a ceasefire. It's possible that Britain was initially willing to accept "pragmatic" but not moral solutions in Cyprus (Kazamias, 2010).

The commander of the Greek air force in his recount of the events to the Prime Minister of Greece claimed that the British informed Athens a few days after the Turkish invasion that British air fighters would intercept and drive away Greek aeroplanes intending to operate in Cyprus at the crucial timespan.[50]

In the post-junta Greece, all political forces held the United Kingdom responsible for the "Cyprus Tragedy". During the first major foreign affairs debate of the new Greek democratic parliament, all main speakers attacked British policy in Cyprus, while the leader of the Panhellenic Socialist Movement Andreas Papandreou forcefully accused Henry Kissinger of being personally responsible for the "slaughter of our brothers in Cyprus". But even the more level-headed Karamanlis stated verbatim ... *at this point, I cannot help stressing Great Britain's responsibilities for the tragedy of Cyprus. Britain, as a guarantor power, and having troops on the spot, had the right and the duty to intervene and prevent both the Athens coup and the Turkish landing. And it did not only have the right, but also the possibility of doing so, because it maintained the necessary military forces within the island. the sequel is already known* ... Interestingly enough, this statement was, as the British embassy bitterly reported, greeted with applause from all sides of the house.[51]

The military and political response of the Greek-Cypriot forces stationed on the island to the Turkish invasion, which sparked numerous theories about whether or not there was a will to oppose the Turkish invasion, is one of the most intriguing parts of the Cyprus Crisis. As a matter of fact, there were some inexplicable shortcomings and decisions that fuelled these theories. For example, it has been asserted that the National Guard had no serious plan for addressing a Turkish invasion except one devised by Georgios Grivas in 1964. At that time, however, Turkey had no landing craft and this had been encapsulated into the plan. Moreover, the existing Greek forces were ineffectively used during the invasion, while large quantities of ammunition never arrived, because they were taken back to Greece by order of the head of the Greek Armed Forces Bonanos (Drousiotis, 2006a, pp. 205–212).

Furthermore, although it should be taken for granted that the overthrow of Makarios and the takeover of the power by a strong anti-Turkish-Cypriot disposed government that was immediately recognised by Athens, would prompt the reaction of Turkey, no military preparations took place. This is quite astonishing given that at the Mersina harbour across Cyprus were taking place extensive military preparations heralding an invasion. Nevertheless, no provision was made for mining potential landing sites and no mines were laid in the respective sea areas. The machine gun positions on the Kyrenia coastline were not manned. Even after the Turkish invasion had already been in full swing, the putschist leadership of the National Guard assured the heads of the various military units facing the Turkish operation that these were just military exercises for power demonstration! (Hellenic Parliament and House of Representatives, 2018, pp. 358–365).

Things, however, seem to be more complicated. The Greek-officered National Guard in Cyprus consisted at the time of 8,500 to 9,000 men and could in a successful mobilisation reach the size of 24,000 men. It was subdivided into five higher tactical commands, to which 15 infantry regiments, with a total strength of about 5,000 men were attached: The armoured cavalry command with one motorised infantry regiment; one medium armoured division and one reconnaissance division; the artillery command with eight artillery squadrons and three independent artillery battalions; the Cyprus naval command with one naval and submarine base at Bogazi, north of Famagusta, two naval Stations at Kyrenia and Paphos, four naval stations; the Cyprus air command with one air base at Lakatamia near Lekosia, two airfield protection squadrons (one at Lakatamia and one at Tymbos) and two control and warning station squadrons (radar) (one at Kormakitis, on the north-western edge and one at Kandara Hill). The range of the radars was approximately 140 nautical miles. Finally, it engulfed the Greek Cypriot military unit of ELDYK, with two infantry regiments of a total strength of about 1,200 men. It possessed with the exception of some modern Belgian weapons (rifles, submachine guns and machine guns), purchased in the last two years, predominantly ageing weapons, of Russian, British, German and American origin, mostly remnants of World War II without replacement components and correlation to each other and practically no air force, although the necessary infrastructure was in place. The anti-air-force and anti-tank defence machinery was also very deficient. Actually, the National Guard was able to carry out a coup but ill-equipped to combat the Turkish modern army, organised in line with NATO standards and the Turkish-Cypriot forces that also had been trained by Turkish officers in the years before. The junta-led commanders of the National Guard were, however, confident that the existing forces were able to repel any Turkish attack "due to the first-class training they had received and despite the despite the sizeable portion of leftists sponsored by the anti-Hellenic disposed Makarios government included".[52]

Regarding the defence plan of Cyprus, it is noteworthy that in 1967, the National Guard reformulated its head goals emphasising the dangers emanating from the Turkish-Cypriot exclaves and the need to embolden the presence of Greek officers (who were expected to be loyal to the military regime in Athens) within the military contingent. According to the estimate of the General Staff of the National Guard, Turkey from 1967 until 1974 continued to organise the Turkish Cypriots along the lines of the regular army (platoons, companies, battalions, regiments), foruming under a General Military Command. The total strength of the Turkish-Cypriot army, in June 1974 ranged from 11,000 to 13,500 men. This force was organised into eight regiments, comprising a total of 27 infantry battalions. In addition to these, there was the TURDYK, with a strength of about 1,000 men, organised in a regiment of two infantry battalions. Against this background, the General Staff of the Greek-Cypriot National Guard devised the new Cyprus

Defence Plan, with the codified title *Aphrodite*, which provided for a main defence effort in the Famagusta area and a secondary one in the Nicosia and Kyrenia area. According to this plan, Cyprus was divided into five sectors, with minor differences from those of the old plan and with the same higher tactical commands. Concerning the planning for repelling a possible landing action, it was decided in April 1968 that the operative deployment of the ELDYK, as the main counter-attack force, and the disposition of a submarine to attack the amphibious forces, two torpedo boats and one squadron of 18 bombing-personnel aircraft.[53] This plan obviously did not work out and the Turkish forces faced only little resistance but there are good reasons for that.

First, it should be kept in mind that the Greek-Cypriot community was at the time of the Turkish invasion plagued by a civil war between Makarios-supporters and Makarios opponents supported by the Greek junta, affecting, if not paralysing at all, the operational capability of the Greek-Cypriot armed forces.

Second, the military regime in Athens, proved to be completely unprepared to detain both the Turkish invasion or a possible Turkish onslaught in the Aegean Sea and in the continental Greek–Turkish borders in northern Greece. Limited attempts to send air and naval reinforcements to Cyprus with a few exceptions ended in total failure. The Greek armed forces were in a bad shape. In December 1968, NATO's Supreme Allied Commander of Europe, General Lauris Norstad, received, upon his request, a report on the political situation in Greece and the Greek army's current condition. The report, authored by Officer Orestis Vidalis, provides insights into the then-Greek military. In Vidalis' assessment, morale, general combat effectiveness and the nation's ability to wage war were, after the miliary coup, severely hampered. The author claims that the dictatorship made significant efforts to silence critics both inside and outside of Greece. The colonels employed public relations specialists in the UK and the US and invited well-known members of the Greek-American community to Greece for "red carpet treatment", who in, return, gave to the dictatorship a lot of support. In the navy and air force, there were very few junta supporters and members, since these branches were monarchists. Additionally, the report says, the junta created a political/security structure in the military that was "completely different from the chain of command" from the unit level to the top. All matters relating to the security objectives of the junta as a political organisation were under the supervision of these units. The people in charge of these units reported through their own channels to the colonels. There were many levels of junta devotion. A few junior officers and low-ranking officers, as well as a tiny number of steadfast junta allies, supported the government. These officers served as the face of the junta's slogans, and received promotions, salary increases, and new responsibilities. Another portion of officers didn't like the regime but were indifferent and came to terms with the status quo. There also were numerous high-ranking officers who vehemently opposed the government but were either neutralised or unable to take any action against it.[54]

In the course of time, the situation deteriorated. On 20 July 1974, a short time after the Turkish invasion, the junta declared a lukewarm general mobilisation of the army (in the navy the mobilisation was more limited) that included a military draft that ended up in a fiasco. Contrary to the dictator Ioannides and the mid-rank officers around him, a significant part of the military leadership opposed the idea of a high-scale war with Turkey. The generals were afraid to risk the Greek sovereignty over the eastern Aegean Greek islands which were vulnerable to a Turkish amphibious operation. With the exception of a number of modem F-4s, which had not been yet fully integrated into the Greek air force, Cyprus was situated beyond the range of Greek aircraft. The dispatch of special raid forces to Cyprus as a surrogate for the absence of the air force did not work due to the chaotic conditions that prevailed in the Greek army and government. The military system of the dictatorship turned out beyond doubt to be, hollow, incoherent and corroded. In the manpower, the situation was even worse. The dictatorship had a disastrous impact on the discipline, morale, and efficiency of the armed forces. The regime had conducted several purges and disposed of "disloyal" competent officers. Although it was a military junta, it had never been espoused by the entire armed forces. The fact that the rebel officers perjured themselves by overthrowing the legitimate government and by arresting their own superior officers, thereby abolishing de facto the established hierarchical structure, created a disastrous precedent. Through the abolishment of legitimate seniority, in the following years tragi-comic development occurred with generals receiving orders from subordinate officers. Moreover, mutual distrust began infiltrating the army due to fear of denunciation for "lack of loyalty" towards the colonels. The remaining loyal to the regime officers lost any credibility with their subordinates and were afraid of the soldiers, especially the recruits who joined the army with the mobilisation and, as a rule, disobeyed them. The open defiance of reservists towards the career officers revealed the anti-regime sentiments of the civilian population (Rizas, 2018, p. 103; Tsiridis & Papanikolopoulos, 2017; Athenian, 1972, pp. 110–111; Diamandouros, 1984, p. 53).

In May 1973, the military junta averted at the very last moment a big mutiny in the navy: 73 military officers (63 of the Greek naval army, five of the land force and five of the air force) and six private citizens, were arrested for being involved in the attempted mutiny. The rebels intended to issue an ultimatum to the dictatorial regime calling for the dismissal of the colonels and the assumption of power by a provisional inter-party government with a view to restoring constitutional order and holding elections. Should the ultimatum not be accepted or remain unanswered, the rebels would occupy the island of Syros and blockade the port of Thessaloniki and possibly the ports of other cities, thus increasing the pressure on the regime. Although the plan was leaked and the mutiny failed, the junta out of fear to turn the entire navy against it, treated most of the arrested rebels with relative leniency. The damage, however, had been done. The military regime had been challenged from within, by its main pillar, the army. A few days after the failed mutiny, the commander of the destroyer Velos, Captain Nikolaos Pappas, together with six other officers and 24 non-commissioned officers who had joined the naval mutiny, split from a NATO military exercise and escaped to Italy where they were granted political asylum (Papadimitriou, 1985; Weltforum Verlag München, 1973, pp. 384–385).

The dramatic events in Cyprus exposed the gigantic flaws in the administration and in the military machinery of the Greek junta. Despite the official propaganda of the return of order into the country, it had been used as justification for the imposition of the regime, in fact, there was a complete lack of organisation and co-ordination through the various instances of the state and the army. This is revealed in the recounts of the commanders of the armed forces to the new democratic government after the break-up of the junta. Despite the obvious attempt to refuse responsibility, it is obvious that all these quirky persons were completely unworthy of the positions they had usurped some years ago and entirely incapable of executing elementary tasks such as transporting small troops or organising the supply of operating forces. During the traumatic events, a lot of hilarious incidents took place. For example, in some cases the warplanes could not even take off due to weird accidents or the poor condition of the runways etc.[55]

The defence expenditures had increased in the period 1967–1974, however, the modernisation of weapon systems was very slow for various reasons. The purchases that had been made in the years 1968 to 1972 were due for delivery in 1977. The two comprehensive five-year armaments plans, initiated by the military regime had already burdened the Greek budget with 1.6 billion US dollars to be paid until

1987, whereas the public debt had already been tripled. In April 1974, and after the US refused to provide more weapons to the regime but only credits, the colonels had proceeded exceptionally into new orders of weapons that would be delivered in the next years: 150 tanks and 105 tracked vehicles, 11 helicopters, frigates and 40 aeroplanes from France and Italy. The defence capabilities of the country, however, were still inadequate. The four guided missile patrol boats received from France had defective missiles. The maintenance capabilities of the planes were also in a very poor state. The anti-aircraft capabilities also were very limited. Greece, however, relied almost exclusively on the United States for the supply of war material and at the time the Greek-American relations were not in the best shape.[56]

The ability of the navy and air force to operate in conjunction with each other was troublesome despite the acquisition in 1972 of four German submarines and four French missile boats. The navy's capabilities were also affected by the mutiny of 1973. The air force was affected less than the other branches, because the colonels did not carry out a massive purge there. The air force, however, could not be supplied with modern aeroplanes because of the US military embargo in the first years of the junta and the fact that the colonels favoured the more loyal infantry. After long negotiations, eventually in the summer of 1974, the regime struck a deal with the French company Dassault for the purchase of Mirage F-1 fighter jets that were to be delivered between 1974 and 1977. Last but not least, due to its militant anticommunism, the regime oriented its defence and deterrence planning towards the Balkan Communist countries and not Turkey (Chourchoulis, 2014, pp. 297–300).

Against this background, the new democratic government of national unity that took over the power from the dictators who had left the army and the public administration in a pile of rubble, was tasked with the challenging duty of defending Cyprus. The new administration immediately rehabilitated some experienced officers who had been side-lined by the dictators and drove out officers still loyal to the colonels' regime who still controlled sizeable units of the army and threatened to overthrow the democratic government (Kourkouvelas, 2014, p. 547). This was a difficult, time-consuming but necessary undertaking although it negatively affected the operational capabilities of the armed forces at a crucial time.

After the failure of the Geneva negotiations, and after the second stage of the invasion, the new administration faced for the first time the likelihood of a full-fledged Greek–Turkish war. On 14 August 1974, Defence Minister Evangelos Averof asked the leadership of the army to inform him a) about the state of the armed forces, b) its ability to deter a Turkish attack in Thrace at the Evros River (the continental Greek–Turkish borders), c) which Aegean islands were regarded as adequately manned and combat-ready.[57] According to the Generals in Thrace, there were stationed an infantry battalion, two medium tank divisions and two companies of tracked vehicles. The armed forces on the islands of Chios, Lemnos, Rhodes, Kos, Lesvos and Samos had been enforced with four infantry battalions and other military units with tanks, artillery and machine guns. The generals estimated that with the proper assistance of the air forces and the adequate functions of tele-communications, those places would provide the necessary defence. However, it was desirable to send further enforcement to the Evros border with local reserves. The fact that a whole division had been reserved for a possible deployment in Cyprus was "an obstacle".[58]

The army, however, was, in reality, disintegrating. The reservists behaved arbitrarily, whereas the regular officers abused the reservists causing more defiance. The Defence Ministry tried to bring some order adopting a new code of conduct for the military personnel.[59] The chief commanders of the army admitted that the general mobilisation had essentially failed. On 12 August, at a meeting on the evaluation of the situation attended by the entire political and military leadership, it was revealed that 270,000 men were initially called to serve, but only 110,000 of them were deemed fit. These joined the existing 117,000. The generals also disclosed the shocking information that it would take one year to successfully complete the draft and three to four years to secure the necessary supplies to make the army ready for war! Karamanlis then asked the generals to explain why before or during the Turkish invasion of Cyprus the National Guard forces were not sufficiently enforced and what was the current situation on the island. The heads of the armed forces, generals Bonannos and Galatsanos, responded that the distance in combination with the superiority of the Turkish air force had hindered the deployment of troops. The 25,000 troops stationed on the island were well-equipped and in principle could mount effective defence but the coup d'état had put them into disarray forcing them to leave their positions. Additionally, the army leaders briefed the government about the current balance of power with Turkey. There was a force ratio of about 1:2 or 1:3. Turkey possessed more warships (destroyers, frigates, cruisers, corvettes, etc.) and submarines. Additionally, the anti-aircraft capacity of the ships was negligible. The balance of power in the air force was also in favour of Turkey which possessed more aeroplanes, helicopters, missiles, radars, refuelling bases, etc. Moreover, some of the air fighters could not be used because the training of the Greek forces had not been completed. All in all, the Turks had a three-to-one advantage over the naval and air force in terms of ships, submarines and aircraft, whereas the supply flow to the armed forces stationed on the islands was not guaranteed. If the traditional enemies of Greece, Bulgaria, refrained from attacking, these forces could launch an attack in Thrace by establishing a bridgehead on Turkish soil. The generals also believed that the Turks would be unable to deploy sizeable forces and take advantage of their numerical superiority towards the islands because a sufficient number of Greek forces had already been deployed and the inhabitants on the islands of Chios, Mytilini, Samos, Kos, Rhodes and Lemnos had been armed. If the Greek forces moved quickly, they could achieve significant blows to the Turkish forces but then it could be difficult to support the attacking forces, whereas such a move would provoke an international outcry. Sending a division to Cyprus would weaken the naval and air forces, while during its transport there could be casualties. Furthermore, this move could compel the great powers to intervene in Cyprus.[60]

Taking into consideration all these factors, it was decided in the middle of August to withdraw the Greek armed forces from Cyprus in order to stop the Turkish forces from further advancing, Later, many castigated Karamanlis for this decision, blaming him for defeatism or indifference.[61] Under these circumstances, however, this was the best he could do and hence this criticism is not justified.

Notes

1 Edward Johnson for example maintains that Turkey actually took over the role against the Soviet Union, Great Britain had sought for itself in the 19th century against the Russian empire and therefore could never antagonise Turkey (Johnson, 2005, pp. 21–22).

2 To the same purpose, the British also tried to make the Greek government "aware of the Turkish Government's concern on Cyprus", Public Record Office (henceforth PRO): CO 926/183: "Telegram from the Secretary of State for the Colonies to the Cyprus Governor, 14 May 1955".

3 From Time to time the British Colonial authorities attempted to tighten control of the educational system in order to contain nationalistic tendencies of the two communities. PRO: CO 67/240/11/12: "Exchange of Telegrams between the Foreign Office and the British Governor in Cyprus 1931"; CO 67 259/10: "Union with Greece-Panhellenic Propaganda in 1935".

4 PRO: CO 67/368/1: "Law to Amend the Elementary Education Laws, 1933–1949".

5 Since the schoolteachers were controlled by local politicians and were dependent upon them for their advancement in their profession, they served usually

the political purposes of their "masters". PRO: CO 67/227/5: "Precis on Nicholson's Dispatch on Cyprus Constitution, 30 January 1929".

6 PRO: SA 02/133: "Report of the British Colonial government to the Foreign Office regarding the actions by the Greek Consul Mavromichalis, April 1878"; CO 67/273/10: "Internal report of the Foreign Office on the Greek King's Involvement in the Cypriot Affairs, December 1937"; CO 67 272/17–18–19, Union with Greece. Exploitation of Athleticism and other Activities for Propaganda Purposes: "Reports of the Cyprus Governor to Foreign Office 1937". Every sport event, in which a Greek athlete participated was celebrated and exploited by ... *who still nurse the dream of Enosis and whose desire it was and it is to strengthen the bonds between Cyprus and Greece ...* In 1937 maps showed up in Cyprus denoting Cyprus as part of Greece.

7 PRO: CO 67/228/1: "Dispatches of the British Embassy in Athens to the Foreign Office, 1929".

8 PRO: CO 67/227/5: "Exchange of Telegrams between the Governor of Cyprus and the Secretary of the State for the Colonies in June–August 1929"; In 1929, a committee of Greek Cypriots went to London to convey to the Great Britain's leadership the grievances of the Cypriot population about the colonial administration and to promote the *Enosis* objective. CO 67/227/5: "Cyprus Governor's Report to the Foreign Office 16 July 1929"; The takeover of power by the Labour Party in 1930 was considered to be conducive for the materialisation of the *Enosis* desire (CO 67/234/1: "Panhellenic Propaganda 1930"). Another distinctive example is the letter sent to the King of the British Empire by the Church or Cypriot organisations abroad on the occasion of coronation of the King George in May 1937 (CO 67/272/19), in which it is stated ... *Cyprus hoping that Great Britain would prove the bridge which should unite her with her mother Greece, has seen with bitterness these hopes not only falsified but also a systematic attempt made by this employees of the home Government in Cyprus, with the tacit consent unfortunately of the Colonial Office, to vitiate the Greek conscience of the inhabitants of the island ...*

9 PRO: CO 67/240/11/12: "Exchange of Telegrams between the Foreign Office and the British Governor in Cyprus in 1931"; CO 67/244/7: "Reports on Panhellenic Propaganda and Union with Greece in 1932". Of course, a considerable portion of the Greek Cypriot Population did not share the ideal of Enosis, was content with its status as subject of the British Crone and just sought to attain more civil liberties. See an example in the collective petition sent to the colonial authorities in 1937 (CO 67/276/18: "Political Situation in Cyprus").

10 PRO: CO 254/6 and 257/34 and 254/7, Panhellenic Propaganda: "Reports of the British Governor in Cyprus 1933–1934"; CO 67/266/13: "Extract from the Monthly Policy Intelligence Report on Cyprus for the month of October 1936"; CO 67/368/7 and 8, Political Situation. Greek interest in Cypriot affairs: "Reports of the Colonial Authorities in Cyprus in 1951"; CO 926/188: Activities of the Greek Consul General in Cyprus 1954–1956"; CO 67 259/11: "Panhellenic Propaganda in 1935"; CO 67 262/2: "Activities of Turkish and Greek Consuls in 1935"; CO 67/266/13: "Activities of Foreign Consuls in 1936"; CO 67 244/7: "Reports of the British Embassy in Athens on Activities by Various Organisations Agitating the Ideal of Enosis in Greece in 1932".

11 PRO: CO 67/266/13: "Extract from the Monthly Policy Intelligence Report on Cyprus for the Month of October 1936"; CO 67 262/2: "Reports on activities of Turkish and Greek Consuls in 1935".

12 PRO: CO 254/5, Political Situation in Cyprus: "Reports of the Governor Palmer April 1934".

13 From the first moment of the British rule, the Church consistently fostered the cause of *Enosis* on the island. Under its auspices, fundraising activities took place to help the Greek Army or various other purposes and fostering the bond between Cyprus and Greece. Therefore, the colonial authorities, in many cases, interfered in the electoral process for the post of Archbishop. For example, persons who had been deported from Cyprus in consequence of seditious activities could not participate in the elections. PRO: CO 67/228/3 and 4: "Dispatches of the Governor in Cyprus to the Foreign Office in 1929"; CO 67/275/10 and 276/1, "December 1937"; CO 67 291/3 and 293/11: "Reports by the Cyprus Governor on Enosis Agitation 1938–39". The commissioner of the police suggested the prohibition of various Greek Orthodox organisations in 1938, while the police was convinced that the Church was behind of many Greek Cypriot pro-Enosis activities that took place in 1939. In some reports of the Cyprus Governor (CO 67/266/13, 5 November 1936), the Church is labelled "Chief Villain".

14 PRO: CO 67/342/2: "Telegram from the Acting Governor of Cyprus to the Secretary of State for the Colonies 30 November 1948".

15 PRO: CO 67/342/1, Turks in Cyprus: "Reports of the Colonial Authorities in Cyprus late 1948–early 1949"; CO 926/183: "Internal Report of the Foreign Office for Mr W. G. Wilson and Mr. Morris 6 June 1954".

16 PRO: CO 67/368/1; CO 67/342/1, Turks in Cyprus: "Interim Report of the Committee for Turkish Affairs, 1949".

17 PRO: CO 67/342/2: "Telegram from the British Embassy in Ankara to the Foreign Office, 9 February 1949" and "Extract from the Political Summary No. 3, 6th–28th February".

18 PRO: CO 67/270/6: "Committee of Imperial Defence. Eastern Mediterranean Understanding with Turkey and Greece, 29 July 1936".

19 PRO: CO 926/183, Turkish interest in the Political situation in Cyprus 1954–1956: "Telegrams from the Colonial Authorities in Cyprus and the British Embassy in Ankara to the Foreign Office in 1954".

20 Konstantinos Papakonstantinou Archive (henceforth cited as Papakonstantinou Archive): Folder 70: "Study of the General Staff of the Greek Cypriot National Guard on the situation in Cyprus, Nicosia 31 May 1974".

21 It is noteworthy that the CIA analysts in Athens feared since April 1967 an attempt by Greek troops in Cyprus to overthrow the President of the Republic, Archbishop Makarios, and to set up a government more compatible with the new regime in Athens, i.e. more hard-nosed and overtly anti-Communist. CIA releases 2017: "CIA Intelligence Memorandum on the Military Takeover April 22 and 26, 1967".

22 PRO: FCO 9/1151: "Reports of British High Commission in Nicosia on the political situation in Cyprus July 1970"; Papakonstantinou Archive: Folder 70: "Study of the General Staff of the Greek Cypriot National Guard on the Situation in Cyprus, Nicosia 31 May 1974"; (Kyrris, 1996, pp. 391–399).

23 Papakonstantinou Archive: Folder 70: "Study of the General Staff of the Greek Cypriot National Guard on the Situation in Cyprus, Nicosia 31 May 1074".

24 Papakonstantinou Archive: folder 70: "Study of the General Staff of the Greek Cypriot National Guard on the situation in Cyprus, Nicosia 31 May 1974".

25 FRUS: Document 382. "Telegram From Secretary of State Rogers to the Department of State New York, October 7, 1971. Memorandum of Conversation: Under Secretary of State Palamas, Ambassador Pesmazotlou; US Secretary of State Sisco, McCloskey and Boyatt"; Document 393. "Memorandum From Harold Saunders and Rosemary Neaher of the National Security Council Staff to the President's Assistant for National Security Affairs (Kissinger) Washington, 10 February 1972, Subject: The Cyprus Situation".

26 National Archives and Records Administration (henceforth cited as NARA): RG 59: General Records of the Department of State 1963–1974: Bureau of Near Eastern and South Asian Affairs, "Confidential Report on Upcoming Meeting with the Greek Ambassador Palamas November 14, 1967"; FRUS: Document 379, "Telegram from the US Embassy to Greece to the Department of State Athens, 7 September 1971, 1620Z, Subject: Cyprus: My Meeting with Palamas following Makarios Visit".

27 NATO Archive: Document PO /70/522: "Secretary General's Greek–Turkish relations *Watching Brief* 23 November 1970"; PO 71/658: "Secretary General's Greek–Turkish relations Watching Brief 29 November 1971".

28 WikiLeaks: "Possible Leak of CIA Memoranda on 1974 Cyprus Crisis 1979 July 16". https://wikileaks.org/plusd/cables/1979ATHENS06261_e.html

29 NARA releases 2005: "Telegram of the US Embassy in Athens to the Secretary of State in Washington, Subject: Foreign Policy Views of Brigadier General Ioannides 14 JUN 1974".

30 Of the 112 officers charged, 21 were tried and 19 convicted. Eight officers received life terms, while Georgios Papadopoulos, the mastermind of the regime, was sentenced to death for sedition. His death sentence was later commuted to life imprisonment.

31 NATO Archive: "NATO confidential Record – MC-30-74. Special Record on the 30th Meeting of the Military Committee in 1974 held on Tuesday, 23 July 1974 at the NATO Headquarters, Brussels, Belgium".

32 NATO Archive: IMSWM-175–74 PD: "Memorandum for the Members of the Military Committee. The Chief, French Military Mission. Subject: Broad Military Implications to NATO from the Cyprus Crisis 1974. Reference: Working Draft Background Paper, 22 July 1974".

33 The new assertive Prime Minister Konstantinos Karamanlis also suspended the facilities provided by the port of Elefsina to the US bases, temporarily suspending the operation of the American base at Elliniko and placing the other NATO bases under a Greek commander. The Turkish government also suspended the operation of all US bases following the imposition of the US arms embargo. The Turkish tactic, however, proved more effective, as the 1976 agreement allowed the bases to reopen by taking various compensations including $250 million in annual rent

(Bredimas, 1986). The official withdrawal was completed two years later, in November 1976. NATO Archive: Record – MC-41–76: "Summary Record on the 41st Meeting of the Military Committee in 1976, held on 10 November 1976 at the NATO Headquarters, Brussels, Belgium".

34 NATO Archive: Confidential Record – RIC-32–74: "Restricted Session on 19 August 1974, the 32nd Meeting of the Military Committee Held on 14 August 1974 at the NATO Headquarters, Brussels".

35 NATO archive: Document PO 72/422 (Revised): "Report of the NATO Secretary General on the watching brief to the ministerial meeting of December 1972, 29 November 1972"; NATO archive: Document PO PO/ 73/160: "Report of the NATO Secretary General on the Watching Brief to the Ministerial Meeting of December 1973".

36 Konstantinos Karamanlis Archive (henceforth cited as Karamanlis Archive): Folder 43, "NATO (June 1979)"; Folder NATO-Greece 20B, 43–352, "Letter from the Prime Minister Karamanlis to the Prime Minister of Denmark, Poul Hartling, 28 August 1974".

37 NATO archive: C-R (74) 44 PD, "Summary Record of a Meeting of the Council Held at the NATO Headquarters in Brussels, on 25 September 1974".

38 NATO archive: Document P0/74/156: "GREEK–TURKISH RELATIONS. Secretary General's Watching Brief, 3 December 1974".

39 PRO: FCO 9/2010, Relations between Greece and Turkey, Dispute over the Aegean Sea: "Telegram of the UK Permanent Mission to the Foreign Office on Greco/Turkish Dispute, 5 June 1974"; "Telegram from the Foreign Office to the UK Mission to NATO, Subject: Greek/Turkish relations: representations to NATO, 17 May 1974".

40 US Department of State released documents in 2005: "Telegram From the US Embassy to NATO to the Secretary of State in Washington 15 August 1974, subject: Greece, NATO, and the US – some reflections".

41 See the documents revealed by the National Herald (2018) on 4 September 2018 available in www.thenationalherald.com/212131/white-house-1974-cyprus-meeting-kissinger-backed-turkey-over-greece/

42 Karamanlis Archive: Folder 20 B NATO-Greece (1974–1978): "Telegram of the Greek Embassy in Washington to the Greek Foreign Ministry August 17, 1974".

43 According to the US Ambassador in Cyprus Ronald I. Spiers in Ankara 1977–1980 many in Congress were motivated by the desire to embarrass Kissinger rather than just to punish Turkey, because Kissinger liked the Turks very much: Library of Congress. The Association for Diplomatic Studies and Training Foreign Affairs Oral History Project, Interview with US Ambassador with Ronald I. Spiers www.loc.gov/item/mfdipbib001109

44 WikiLeaks: https://wikileaks.org/plusd/cables/1978ATHENS01377_d.html. "US Department of State. Defense Minister Discusses Nuclear Weapons in Greece Control of US bases, and Charges of American Military Interference in Cyprus Crisis During Parliamentary Interpellation, 15 February 1978".

45 PRO: FCO 9/2010, Relations between Greece and Turkey, Dispute over the Aegean Sea: "Telegram of the Foreign Office to the UK Permanent Mission to NATO and to the British Embassies to Athens, Ankara and Nicosia, 5 July 1974".

46 NATO Archive: "Confidential Record – RIC-32–74 (Restricted Session) 19 August 1974 on the 32nd Meeting of the Military Committee held on 14 August 1974 at the NATO Headquarters, Brussels, Belgium".

47 Papakonstantinou Archive: Folder 70: "Study of the General Staff of the Greek Cypriot National Guard on the Situation in Cyprus, Nicosia 31 May 1974".

48 Karamanlis Archive: Folder 4B, "Petros Arapakis Recounts to Prime Minister Konstantinos Karamanlis on the Events that Brought About the Transition to the New Government on 23 July 1974, Athens 17 April 1975", "Alexandros Papanikolaou Recounts to Prime Minister Konstantinos Karamanlis (1975)"; (Drousiotis, 2006, pp. 188–189 and 223–225).

49 US Department of State released documents in 2005: "Telegram from the US Mission to NATO to the Secretary of State in Washington 13 May 1974, Subject: U.S. Policy towards Greece".

50 Karamanlis Archive: Folder 4B, "Alexandros Papanikolaou Recounts to Prime Minister Konstantinos Karamanlis (1975)".

51 PRO: FCO 9/2012 Relations between Greece and Turkey Dispute over Aegean Sea, "Telegram from the British Embassy in Athens to the Foreign Office 11 February 1975".

52 Papakonstantinou Archive: Folder 70: "Study of the General Staff of the Greek Cypriot National Guard on the Situation in Cyprus, Nicosia 31 May 1974".

53 Ibidem.

54 Lauris Norstad Papers: Box 129, "Vidalis' Personal and Confidential Report for General Norstad, 13 December 1968".

55 Karamanlis Archive: Folder 4B, "Petros Arapakis Recounts to Prime Minister Konstantinos Karamanlis on the Events that Brought About The Transition to the New Government on 23 July 1974, Athens 17 April 1975", "Alexandros Papanikolaou Recounts to Prime Minister Konstantinos Karamanlis (1975)".

56 Averof archive: Folder 28, "Observations of the Hellenic Defence Ministry on the two Five-Year Armament Plans, 4 September 1974"; Karamanlis Archive: Folder 40 (issues of national Defence), "Greece's Armament Program of 1974".

57 Averof Archive: Folder A 24, Subfolders 1–9: "Official Letter from the Defence Minister to the Commander in Chief of the Army and the Special Forces, 14 August 1974".

58 Averof Archive: Folder A 24, Subfolders 1–9: "Reply of the Commander in Chief of the Greek Armed Forces General Greogorios Bonnanos to Averof's letter, 16 August 1974".

59 Averof Archive: Folder A 24, Subfolders 1–9: "Note of the Defence Ministry on the Conditions in the Greek Army, 14 August 1974".

60 Archive of Evangelos Averof: Folder A 24, Subfolders 1–9: "Note of the Bureau of the Defence Minister on the Meeting of 12 August, Athens 25 Augusta 1974"; (Papachelas, 2021, pp. 508–513 and 522–523).

61 This was the accusation directed to Karamanlis during the official investigation inside the Hellenic Parliament by the end of the 1980s, known as the Fakelos tis Kyprou (Cyprus File) by the Greek Socialists and Communists and reproduced later by many across the political spectrum (Hellenic Parliament and House of Representatives, 2018, pp. 11–18).

References

Primary Sources

Archive of Evangelos Averof, Greece's Defence Minister (cited as Averof Archive)
Archive of Konstantinos Karamanlis, Prime Minister of Greece (cited as Karamanlis Archive), unpublished documents.
Dwight Eisenhower Library and Archives: Lauris Norstad (NATO SACEUR) papers and collection (cited as Lauris Norstad papers).
Hellenic Parliament and House of Representatives, 2018. Fakelos tis Kyprou [Cyprus Gate], Vol. ⊠ The Findings. Athens-Nicosia.
Foreign Relations of the United States, 1969–1976, Volume XXIX, Eastern Mediterranean, 1969–1972 (cited as FRUS). US Department of State Office of the Historian, Bureau of Public Affairs United States Government Printing Office, Washington, 2008.
Konstantinos Papakonstantinou Archive (cited as Papakonstantinou Archive)
Library of Congress. The Association for Diplomatic Studies and Training Foreign Affairs Oral History Project.
National Archives and Records Administration (cited as NARA): RG 59: General Records of the Department of State 1963–1974: Bureau of Near Eastern and South Asian Affairs.
Public Record Office (PRO)
US Department of State Releases of Documents in 2005 and 2006.
Wikileaks
NATO Archive

Secondary Sources

Antonopoulos, A. 2016. *Redefining an Alliance: Greek-US Relations, 1974–1980*. PhD thesis submitted at the Department of History of the University of Edinburgh.
Asmussen, J., 2008. *Cyprus At War. Diplomacy and Conflict during the 1974 Crisis*. London: Tauris.
Athenian, 1972. *Inside the Colonels Greece*. London: Chatto and Windus.
Bozarslan, H., 2004. *Istoria tis Sygchronis Tourkias [Histoire de la Turquie Contemporaine]*. Athens: Savvalas Publisher.
Bredimas, A., 1986. Oi Amerikanikes Vaseis stin Ellada [The US military bases in Greece]. In G. Valinakis & P. Kitsos (eds.), *Ellinika Amyntika Provlimata [Greece's Defence Problems]* (pp. 41–90), Athens: Papazisis Publisher.
Chourchoulis, D. 2014. To Zitima ton Stratiotikon Dynatotiton tis Elladas 1967–1974. Esoterikes kai Diethneis diastaseis [Greece's military capabilities 1967–1974. Domestic and International Dimensions]. In *Colonels*

Dictatorship and the Restoration of Democracy. Conference Proceedings (pp. 285–312). Athens: Hellenic Parliament Foundation,.

Diamandouros, N., 1984. Transition to, and consolidation of, democratic politics in Greece, 1974–1983: A tentative assessment. In: G. Pridham (ed.), *The New Mediterranean Democracies: Regime Transition in Spain, Greece and Portugal* (pp. 50–71). London: Frank Cass.

Drousiotis, M., 2006a. *Cyprus 1974. Greek Coup and Turkish Invasion.* Peleus Monographien Reihe zur Archäologie and Geschichte Zyperns Bd. 32. Mannheim and Möhnesee: Bibliopolis.

Drousiotis, M., 2006b. The Greco-Turkish "para-state" in Cyprus 1947–1960. In H. Faustmann and N. Peristianis (eds.), *Britain in Cyprus. Colonialism and Post-Colonialism 1878–2006* (pp. 211–232). Peleus zur Archäologie and Geschichte Zyperns Bd. 19. Mannheim and Möhnesee: Bibliopolis.

Drousiotis, M., 2014. *Kypros 1974–1977. H eisvoli kai oi megales dynameis. H realpolitik ton HPA kai to diplo paixnidi tis ESSD* [*Cyprus 1974–1977. The Invasion and the Great Powers. US Realpolitik and USSR's Double Game*]. Nicosia: Alfadi publisher.

Faustmann, H., 2004. Conflicting nationalisms during British rule and in pre-1974 Cyprus. In R. Stupperich (ed.), *Nova Graecia. Festschrift für Heinz Richter* (pp. 205–220). Mannheim-Möhnesee: Bibliopolis.

Firat, M., 2012. *Oi Tourkoellinikes Scheseis kai to Kypriako* [*The Turkish–Greek relations and the Cyprus problem*]. Athens: Sideris Publisher.

Göktepe, C., 2005. The Cyprus Crisis of 1967 and its Effects on Turkey's Foreign Relations, *Middle Eastern Studies*, 41 (3), 431–444.

Hatzivassiliou, E., 2002. *The Cyprus Question, 1878–1960. The Constitutional Aspect*. Minnesota Mediterranean and East European Monographs XI. Minneapolis: University of Minnesota.

Hatzivassiliou, E., 2020. Bon pour l' Orient. To Zitima tis entaxis tis Kyprou sto NATO 1959–1963 [The issue of Cyprus's accession to NATO 1959–1963]. *Deltos*, vol. 7, 101–124.

Hitchens, C., 2001. *The Trial of Henry Kissinger*. London and New York: Verso.

Johnson, E., 2005. British strategic interests and enosis in colonial Cyprus, in M. Michael and A. Tamis (eds.), *Cyprus in the Modern World* (pp. 13–24). Thessaloniki: Vanias.

Işiksal, H., 2015. The Four Stages of Turkish Position in Cyprus: The Elements of Continuity and Change. In, Örmeci, O, Işiksal. H., et al. (eds.), *Turkish Foreign Policy in the New Millennium* (pp. 297–364). Bern: Peter Lang GmbH, Internationaler Verlag der Wissenschaften,.

Kadritzke, N., & Wagner, W. 1976. *Im Fadenkreuz der NATO. Ermittlungen am Beispiel Cypern*. Berlin: Rotbuch Verlag.

Kaminis, G., 2014. I Apokatastasi tis Dimokratias. Mia Sintagmatiki apotimisi 40 chronia meta [The restoration of democracy. A constitutional appraisal 40 years later]. In *Colonels Dictatorship and the Restoration of Democracy. Conference Proceedings* (pp. 499–502). Athens: Hellenic Parliament Foundation,.

Kazamias, G., 2010. From pragmatism to idealism to failure: Britain in the Cyprus crisis of 1974. *GreeSE Paper No 42 Hellenic Observatory Papers on Greece and Southeast Europe*. www.lse.ac.uk/Hellenic-Observatory/Assets/Documents/Publications/GreeSE-Papers/GreeSE-No42.pdf

Ker-Lindsay, J. 2004. *Britain and the Cyprus Crisis 1963–1964*. Peleus Monographien Reihe zur Archäologie and Geschichte Zyperns Bd. 27. Bibliopolis: Mannheim and Möhnesee.

Ker-Lindsay, J., 2011. *The Cyprus Problem: What Everyone Needs to Know*. Oxford: Oxford University Press.

Kourkouvelas, L., 2014. Synecheia kai Allagi. Oi Kyverniseis Karamanli apenanti stous nostalgous tis Xountas [Continuity and Change. Karamanlis' administrations against the nostalgics of the Junta]. In Hellenic Parliament Foundation (ed.), *I Diktatoria ton Syntagmatarchon kai I apokatastasi tis Dimokratias [Colonels Dictatorship and the restoration of Democracy. Conference Proceedings]* (pp. 545–562). Athens: Hellenic Parliament Foundation.

Kyrris, C., 1996. *History of Cyprus*. Nicosia: Lampousa Publications.

Mallinson, W., 2016. *Kissinger and the Invasion of Cyprus: Diplomacy in the Eastern Mediterranean*. Cambridge: Cambridge Scholars Publishing.

Mallinson, W., & Fouskas, V., 2017. Kissinger and the Business of Government: The Invasion of Cyprus, 15 July–20 August 1974. *Cyprus Review*, 29, 111–134.

Markides, D., 2002. Sir Arthur Clark and the Thirteen Points: International Diplomacy and the Constitutional Crisis: Cyprus 1960–1963. In J. Charalambous*et al.* (eds.), *Cyprus: 40 Years from Independence. Conference Proceedings* (pp. 49–59). Bibliopolis: Mannheim and Möhnesee.

Moustakis, F., 2003. *The Greek–Turkish relationship and NATO*. London: Frank Cass Publishers.

O'Malley, B., & Craig, I., 2001. *The Cyprus Conspiracy. America, Espionage and the Turkish Invasion*. London and New York: I.B. Tauris Publishers.

Papachelas, A., 2021. *Ena Skoteino Domatio 1967–1974 [A Dark Room 1967–1974]*. Athens: Metechmio Publisher.

Papadimitriou, N., 1985. *To kinima tou politikou Naftikou: Maios 1973 [The Greek naval mutiny: May 1973]*. Athens: Elliniki Evroekdotiki Publisher.

Persianis, P., 2006. *Sygkritiki Istoria tis Ekpedefsis tis Kyprou 1800–2004* [Comparative History of Cyprus's Education 1800–2004]. Athens: Gutenberg publisher.

Richter, H., 2007. *Geschichte der Insel Zypern 1959–1965*. Peleus Monographien Reihe zur Archäologie and Geschichte Zyperns. Bd. 37. Wiesbaden: Franz Philipp Rutzen.

Richter, H., 2009. *Geschichte der Insel Zypern 1965–1977*. Peleus Monographien Reihe zur Archäologie and Geschichte Zyperns Bd. 41 (Teil 1). Wiesbaden: Franz Philipp Rutzen.

Rizas, S., 2002/2003. The Greek military regime's policy towards Cyprus, 1967–1974. *Modern Greek Studies Yearbook*, 18/19, 239–252.

Rizas, S., 2018. *Realism and Human Rights in US Policy toward Greece, Turkey, and Cyprus.* Lanham: Lexington Books.

Soulioti, S., 2006. *Fettered Independence. Cyprus, 1878–1964. Vol. I: The Narrative.* Minnesota Mediterranean and East European Monographs XVI. Minneapolis: University of Minnesota.

Stefanidis, I., 1999. *Isle of Discord. Nationalism, Imperialism and the Making of the Cyprus Problem.* New York: New York University Press.

Stergiou, A., 2021. *Greece's Ostpolitik. Dealing With the "Devil".* Contribution to the International Relations. Switzerland AG: Springer Nature.

Theodorakopoulos, P., 1996. *To Kongreso sti Diamorfosi tis Amerikanikis Exoterikis Politikis. O Rolos tou stin periptosi tis Elladas* [*The Impact of the US Congress on the Making of the US Foreign Policy. Its Role in the Case of Greece*]. Athens: Sideris Publisher.

The National Herald, 2018, White House 1974 Cyprus meeting: Kissinger backed Turkey over Greece, 4 September 2018.

Tsardanidis, Ch., 1988. *The Politics of the EEC-Cyprus Association Agreement: 1972–1982.* Nicosia: The Social Research Center.

Tsiridis, G., & Papanikolopoulos, D., 2017. Epistratefsi 1974: o katalytikos rolos ton epistraton stin katarefsi tis diktatorias ton syntagmatarchon [The military draft of 1974. The decisive role of the conscripts in the disintegration of the colonel's regime]. *Hellenic Revue of Political Science*, 42, 203–228.

United Nations Department of Public Information, 1974. *Yearbook of the United Nations.* https://digitallibrary.un.org/record/858832?ln=en

Weltforum Verlag München, 1973. *Weltgeschehen. Internationales Europaforum Juli–September 1973.* München: Weltforum.

2 The Greek–Turkish dispute over the Aegean Sea in the 1970s

The oil crisis in the mid-1970s, which hit Greece and Turkey particularly hard, created another field of contestation between the two nations. In 1973, a large number of speculative news items in the Greek press pinpointed the discovery of commercially exploitable hydrocarbons off the island of Thasos in the northern Aegean by the Denver, Colorado-based Oceanic Exploration Company that had been given a permit by the Greek government to conduct hydrocarbon exploration in the Aegean Sea. The agreement had been signed in 1969 and, under its terms, the company, one of the 27 applications by foreign-based oil exploration companies received by the Greek government, automatically became the lessee of the concession area for 26 years. The concession area was theoretically 50 km^2 but, under certain conditions, could be extended to 100 km^2. In February 1974, the military regime's Prime Minister Androutsopoulos, and the Minister of Industry, Kypraios, officially announced the discovery of a commercially important volume of as much as 50,000 barrels per day, though only 3,000 barrels per day had been proved so far.[1]

The Greek state started conducting explorations in the Aegean in the late 1930s and increased its efforts in the early 1960s, when it gave oil exploration permits to several big foreign oil corporations (ESSO, TEXACO, BP, Oceanic, etc.). Drilling operations for 68 wells started after extensive geology studies generated around 12,200 km of seismic lines. Only the south Kavala gas field and the Prinos oil field turned out to be profitable. Significant hydrocarbon reserves were also found in other wells (Aitoliko, Zakynthos, Thermaikos, etc.) (Lie et al., 2014; Zafiropoulos, 2012).

These licences, according to Alexis Heraclides, allowed for seabed explorations outside of Greek national waters. Based on its interpretation of the pertinent section of the Geneva Convention on the Continental Shelf (1958), which grants the continental shelf to islands,

DOI: 10.4324/9781003350033-3

Greece unilaterally delineated the Aegean continental shelf in this region. In this regard, Heraclides speculates that Athens erroneously believed that the entire Aegean seabed to the west of its eastern islands could only be Greek. This belief was based on the assumption that all of the Aegean Sea's islands, including those that were extremely close to Turkey, enjoyed "full effect" on the delimitation of maritime zones. After that, it started de facto defining the continental shelf. However, Turkey did not respond right away, most likely because until the autumn of 1973 had not faced an urgent need for alternative sources of supply and did not believe that considerable quantities of oil were to be found in the respective exploration areas (Heraclides, 2010, pp. 78–79).

After the announcement of the Greek government, the British embassy in Athens estimated that both the Greek press and state officials exaggerated the prospects of this exploration effort, although it did seem quite possible, perhaps even probable, that some commercially exploitable quantity of oil would be proven in the seas near Thasos. The Legislative Decree of 1969 on research, exploration and exploitation of hydrocarbons in liquid or gaseous stats, the legal basis of the permits provided that ... *the State shall have the exclusive right of research and exploitation of all minerals including hydrocarbons in solid, liquid or gaseous state as well as quarry products which are found on or under the seabed in Greek territorial waters; (b) on or under the sea bed beyond Greek territorial waters, which is an extension of or lies next to the coast of the Greek mainland or the islands at a depth of 200 m from the surface of the sea or even further wherever the overlying waters permit research or exploitation.* There were indications from secret sources that the Greek regime was concerned about possible Turkish attitudes to any discoveries which would result either in an attempt to reinterpret the Lausanne and Montreux Agreements, or to the naked use of superior force.[2]

Even the speculation of the existence of hydrocarbons in the northern Aegean was enough reason to push Turkey into a series of actions. In November 1973, at the highlight of the oil crisis, Turkey granted mineral exploration permits to the Turkish state-run Petroleum company for investigations in 27 marine regions of the eastern Aegean Sea. Additionally, a map illustrating the separation of several continental shelves in the Aegean that took the presence of the Greek islands into consideration was published in the *Turkish Official Gazette*. A median line that is equally spaced from the Greek and Turkish mainland, beginning at the mouth of the Evros River in the north and extending southward from the west of the Greek Islands of the eastern

Aegean, was utilised on the map as a technique of delineating the seabed between Greece and Turkey. This unilateral delimitation of the continental shelf did not engulf the islands, although some of the exploration areas lay just beyond the territorial waters of the large and populated Greek islands of Lesvos, Chios, Lemnos and Samothrace (Syrigos, 2016, pp. 330–332).

Greece lodged diplomatic objections to Ankara, and Turkey responded by saying it would continue its exploratory drilling. By concurrently sending a list of topics for negotiation to Athens that included, among other things, the demilitarisation of the Greek islands, the territorial waters, the Aegean shelf, etc., it also issued additional exploration licences. Athens responded with its own list of issues to be negotiated on. Armed forces of both countries went on alert (Hale, 2013, pp. 115–116).

More precisely, on 7 February 1974, the Greek government filed a Note Verbale, disputing the legality of the permits issued by Turkey and reserving its sovereign rights over the continental shelf bordering the shores of the aforementioned islands. It argued that a median line was necessary to draw an equidistant boundary between the two states' continental shelves. The Greek islands, which are quite near to the Turkish coast, do not have their own shelf, hence the principle of equidistance was not relevant, the Turkish government said in a Note Verbale dated 27 February 1974. The Greek government backed a delimitation based on the terms of the 1958 Geneva Convention on the Continental Shelf in its revised reply of 24 May 1974. The Turkish government responded with a fresh statement indicating its willingness to engage in talks to determine the two nations' shared continental shelf. The Turkish memorandum contained legal arguments that drew upon the 1969 decision of the International Court,[3] introducing the view that agreement between the two states would be a better method of deciding the underwater border than the principle of equidistance which was responded to by the military regime in a rather undiplomatic way. Athens, on the other side, made clear that it claimed a 12-mile stretch of territorial sea. According to the British embassy in Athens, there was a faction in the Greek government around Ioannides, which was "bound to confrontation with the Turks in all matters".[4]

Since at the time negotiations between the UK and France were held on the status of the Channel Islands and the *Third Conference on the Law of the Sea* was unfolding,[5] in which Athens and Ankara exchanged their divergent perceptions on maritime boundaries, both Greeks and Turks contacted British officials to inform them about their positions in the negotiations on the new law of the sea that were about to take place in Karakas. The Turks wanted to know why the British could not make the Channel Islands an enclave within a French continental shelf and make a median line between the UK and France the boundary, thereby ignoring the islands. This approach that also was the Turkish approach for the demarcation of the Aegean continental shelf, e.g. the drawing of a median line between the Greek and the Turkish continental shelf disregarding the island on the "Turkish side" did not, however, resonate well with the British.[6]

The Turks were, however, adamant that the Greek–Turkish case was based on the Aegean being an exceptional case and the only possible way to settle it was by bilateral negotiations. Islands could indeed have continental shelves and the Turkish government did not argue that even those islands sitting on the mainland shelf that was "an obvious prolongation of the Anatolian region" should not be granted one, but that the size of such shelves should be defined by negotiation. Greece and Turkey were allies after all. The Turks felt very sure of their understanding of the topography of the whole Anatolian region in international fora and decided to rely on this in scientific research. They also believed that the recent (1969) Hague judgement on the North Sea enforced the argument about the prolongation of the mainland and the acceptance of special cases. According to the Turkish side, the subject of the continental shelf of course was extremely important in itself but was inevitably linked to the question of the 12-mile territorial waters limit. If the present difference of opinion between Turkey and Greece was only about the continental shelf, it could all be in a lower key. Every sea has its own characteristics. The Aegean Sea, which is a closed sea enabling passage from the Black Sea to the Mediterranean and which has different geological character-istics, was certainly not the same as the Atlantic. If the territorial waters, however, were increased to 12 miles, "the Aegean would become part of Greek territory" and therefore Turkey would never accept increasing the territorial waters to 12 miles in the Aegean. Obviously, Turkish military authorities regarded the Aegean as stra-tegically of the greatest importance for the defence of Anatolia and hence they should have completely free access to it to carry out normal naval defence activity and to keep an eye on Russian move-ments. They were dissatisfied with the existence of the Greek islands on their doorstep and there was always the likelihood to be pushing for adjustment, although the British diplomatic authorities in Turkey downplayed this option in the foreseeable future. According to the British, the Turkish case did not have much support in international law but the claim that the Aegean must be treated as a special case, backed by their insistence that they were open to discussing any suggestions, did not seem so unreasonable. For this reason, the Canadian Ambassador in Ankara was convinced that the best and possibly only solution to the problem might lie in joint exploration and joint participation by the Turks and Greeks in the whole area. There were some Turkish politicians who also would opt for such a scenario.[7]

Henry Kissinger first considered the idea of an Aegean "condominium" between Turkey and Greece, where American interests and businesses would also be included, after learning about the issue from Turan Güneş, the Turkish Foreign Minister. Turkish policy became US policy, and the US formally proposed this to the then-Greek dictator Ioannides. However, Ioannides' regime rejected the idea, claiming that the only area that needed delimitation was between the Turkish coastline and the Greek islands of the eastern Aegean (Papachelas, 2021, pp. 221–242).

It is remarkable that the British put themselves to the trouble to study meticulously all treaties and agreements signed between Greece and Turkey or between the two countries and third countries related to the legal status of the Aegean and to map out the difference. Among others, they came to the conclusion that the map of the *Treaty of Lausanne* actually showed a broken line between the Greek islands and the Turkish mainland, which appears to have been drawn through the mid-point of the channels separating them. Other than this the Greeks claimed territorial waters of 6 miles around their island possessions, and around the mainland, while the rest of the Aegean was international waters. Both Greece and Turkey appeared at that time to have regarded the territorial settlement made at Lausanne as final, and agreements affirming the inviolability of the common frontier were made in the 1930s.[8]

Other British diplomatic reports showed that in the Turkish view of the continental shelf and the Aegean the general provisions of the 1958 Geneva Convention (Article 1) were acceptable. This means that the Turks theoretically accepted that both land masses and islands have continental shelves, because otherwise they would not deny that the United Kingdom has its own shelf. But since the application of Article 1 to the Aegean would turn it into a Greek lake, which the Turks claimed it was the Greek position and aim, they argued that Article 1 of the Geneva Convention was modified by Article 6. The latter defines three principles in cases of dispute between adjacent countries as to the application of Article 1. These are: (a) agreement between the disputants; (b) the recognition of special cases; and (c) the application of the principle of equidistance if agreement on (a) and (b) cannot be reached. Their second basis is the principle of equity (political, economic, etc). At this point, the Turks claimed they were backed up by the International Court in the Hague Advisory opinion on the North Sea. Against this background, the Turks were expected to argue that the Aegean Sea was a special case and that agreement on sovereignty, the continental shelf and the division of spoils, should be reached between the two sides on a basis of equity, e.g. through the application of the third principle of the Article 6, equidistance. This principle legitimised, according to the Turks, their granting of oil exploration rights and therefore a recourse to the International Court of The Hague was not ruled out. So, the essential argument was about sovereignty not about oil and other resources which was secondary, although increasingly acute due to the oil crisis. Apart from it, the discovery of oil at Thassos created the prospect of the existence of oil in the rest of the Aegean and brought the possibility of confrontation nearer. Two views stood against each other:

From the Turkish point of view, there were really three aspects to the Aegean: (1) oil; (2) other natural resources: fishing and some other minerals such as magnesium; (3) strategic. The actual problems arising from these separate into two: (a) the division of the resources (and hence the geography) of the seabed and continental shelf; (b) the limits of territorial waters especially around the islands. Turkey should have that part of the continental shelf extending from their coast up to a line joining points of greatest depth in the Aegean Sea, while special arrangements would need to be made in the areas around the Greek islands. If the line of greatest depth in the Aegean were taken as a border between the Greek and Turkish seabed, then the Turkish area would come very close to Thasos and the Mount Athos peninsula. The formal Greek position depended upon Athens' interpretation of Article 1 of the 1958 Geneva Convention which provides for the continental shelf to include the seabed and subsoil of similar depth adjacent to the coasts of islands. This principle, according to the British, would give Greece rights over almost all of the Aegean Sea and would, perhaps, be difficult to retain. On the other hand, the "line of greatest depth approach", along the Thracian line, as this had been tested elsewhere, would produce very different results in the Aegean. On the islands, the present Greek territorial waters extended for 6 miles, unless this would encroach upon Turkish territorial waters, in which case the mid-point of the channel between the coast and the island was the limit of Greek waters. The Turks feared that the Greeks proposed to extend their territorial waters to a limit of 12 miles around their islands. This would hamper Turkish naval movements and possibly their egress from the Aegean Sea. The Greek government seemed to have no intention of raising this issue in the negotiations with the Turks, although it was a matter of national sovereignty. Athens also planned to warn off the international companies (presumably American) that would take on the drilling activities on behalf of the Turks, as it believed that the Turks had no resources of their own to undertake this kind of work. Since both sides took an equally hard-line in this matter, Greek–Turkish relations appeared to be heading to an impasse.[9]

The state of the Muslim minority in Greece was an additional matter of concern for the British as it was feared that could compound the rekindled tensions over the Aegen. In January 1974, the British Ambassador visited northern Greece where the Muslim minority lived to get an idea of the situation there. Overall, he formed the view that the "Turkish minority" was materially comfortable, but extremely limited by a combination of their own failure to integrate into the Greek machine, and local Greek discrimination and control (for example, the purchase of cars, was obstructed by bureaucratic requirements, which they find hard to fulfil, their newspapers were censored etc.). The Turkish government was, according to the Ambassador's report, careful to avoid any provocation and its stated position, in which it fully accepted the integration of the minority within Greece, was admirable. But both locally in Thrace and, domestically it was under (perhaps ill-judged) pressure to do something about it and if Greek/Turkish relations worsened overall, it might well change their policy. The area was primarily of military interest to the Greek government in Athens and, in British Ambassador's view, it would be worthwhile for the military authorities that controlled the area to modify their administrative practices, even at some inconvenience to themselves, in the interest of improved relations with Ankara.[10]

The minorities issue is the oldest aspect of the Greek–Turkish conflict and its origins date back to the advent of the 20th century. Following the Greek–Turkish war (1919–1922), the new Turkish leadership insisted on an exchange of population with Greece as a means of building a nationally homogeneous new Turkish state in place of the multiethnic multi-Ottoman empire. As a result of the *Lausanne Treaty*, however, from the exchange of the population were exempted the Greeks who lived in Istanbul (around 110,000) and the Muslim community living in Western Thrace numbering 120,000 (regarded by Turkey as part of the Turkish diaspora), while the islands inhabited overwhelmingly by Greeks of Imbros and Tenedos at the entrance of Dardanelles would come under special administration by Turkey and a locally recruited police force. In the course of the years, Greece and Turkey blamed each other for not respecting the provisions and modalities of the *Lausanne Treaty*. Indeed, both countries embarked on a plethora of violations of Article 45 of the *Lausanne Treaty*, discrimination of all kinds, harassment, expropriation of land properties in the public interest etc., justified by the principle of reciprocity, which, notably, is a very controversial act in international law.[11] This rule was brutally applied in 1927 and in 1964 after the bicommunal riots in Cyprus and the reckless policy of Makarios, when the Turkish state decided to expel 12,000 Greek citizens from Istanbul and impose a very restrictive regime for those who remained there. To this Greece responded with the removal of citizenship from at least 64,000 members of the Thracian minority from 1964 to 1988 (Tsitselikis, 2006).

The explosive situation in the Greek-Turkish relations further escalated during a NATO military drill in March 1974 held in the north-east Aegean, when Athens refused to grant permission to Turkish aeroplanes to enter the Athens FIR region as a protest against a Turkish ship that had detached itself from the exercise. Turkish ships split from the NATO formation and conducted drills with only the Turkish national military forces, while Turkish military aeroplanes violated Greece's national air space. Eventually, the Greek ships withdrew from the military drill entirely. The incident was the most serious of its kind involving Greek and Turkish forces after a considerable time heralding a deterioration of their bilateral relations that were already under severe strain over Cyprus, Aegean oil, the continental shelf and minorities.[12]

By the end of May 1974, the tensions began to culminate, when Ankara decided to send the oceanographic craft vessel Candarli into the Aegean in order to conduct exploration in areas that extended further west and south, including one that overlapped with a Greek potential continental shelf around the Dodecanese islands. Turkish warships were prominently present during the expedition. The Greek armed forces in northern Greece were alerted and a fighter aircraft was moved to Thessaloniki. The American diplomatic authorities in Greece were also alerted out of fear of a possible escalation, although the Greek government assured the US ambassador that it would remain "cool-headed".[13]

Ankara also assured that the Turkish fleet had a protective role for the Candarli ship, and it was not meant to be a threat. It was merely a matter of utilisation of rights under international and national law.

The national oil company was afraid that it could be harassed while conducting a survey, but the Turkish navy, the Turks asserted, would certainly act very calmly against any provocation or disturbance. Such naval duty was normal and the Turkish government had not considered it necessary to issue a statement about it. However, the British embassy in Ankara had information that the Turkish Army had cancelled all leave for military personnel and all officers were ordered to return to duty. There were again also inflammatory articles in the Turkish press about alleged actions by the Greek government against the minority Muslim minority in Thrace and the building up of Greek forces on the border. The Turkish government was called to "finally adopt a firm line in defence of Turkey's rights and interests which over the years had gradually been eroded".[14]

At the same time, Athens officially asked the British government to warn off British firms with the necessary capability of giving any assistance to the Turks in drilling in disputed areas or in the necessary preliminaries. It was estimated that Turkey lacked the technology and resources to conduct drilling on its own. The same request was lodged to all countries in possession of the necessary technology: France, the Netherlands, Japan, Germany, Italy and the Soviet Union. The US Ambassador, however, informed the Greek Foreign Ministry that the US government could not impose restrictions on survey or drilling operations by US firms but that it could (and on occasion had) issue warnings to firms regarding the difficulties they were likely to encounter if they engaged in such activities in disputed areas. The Canadian government appeared to take the same stance to the Greek appeal and avoid siding with one party whatsoever, thereby prejudging the issue before negotiations had started. The fear of being charged with partiality in the Aegean dispute shaped the United Kingdom's attitude as well, although Greek Foreign Ministry officials conveyed to the British the opinion that it was surely their duty to take sides in the matter and to form a view of the rights and wrongs of the dispute. Nevertheless, Whitehall persistently maintained a course of impartiality in the Aegean maritime dispute, although the experts of the Foreign Office had a complete view of the validity of the arguments on both sides about mineral exploration rights in the Aegean Sea.[15]

On 5 June 1974, the British embassy in Athens sent a cable to the Foreign Office that it had received information from the US embassy that their reconnaissance confirmed the course of Turkish survey vessels and their location between the Greek islands Lesvos and Limnos. They were shadowed by a Greek destroyer escort and Greek maritime reconnaissance aircraft. As seen from the British embassy, the Greek government, after encouraging public interest and belligerent statements for several months, had now had its bluff called and had backed down, at least so far as the survey vessel was concerned. Both sides were still on what was potentially a collision course over an issue in which they had taken mutually irreconcilable positions.[16]

In a bid to calm spirits, some days later the Prime Ministers of the two countries made some conciliatory statements ahead of the NATO summit in Ottawa. However, the CIA estimated that the Aegean dispute would undoubtedly drag on indefinitely, although neither country wanted hostilities.[17]

Only a week later, tensions re-emerged due to inflammatory newspaper publications based on rumours and the assertive Turkish reply to the Greek Note regarding Turkish rights in the Aegean. The Turkish Note rejected the Greek proposal that the talks should be contained strictly within the framework of the 1958 Geneva Agreement, suggesting, instead that negotiations to settle the dispute should begin without any preconditions. At the same time the newspaper *Gunaydin* published a map, drawn up by the International Petroleum Company, purporting to show the proposed division of the English Channel's seabed in a way favourable to the Turkish interests: An island unless it is a state does not generate its own shelf and when the division of seabed between two states is decided according to the median, the islands should be ignored. For this reason, the British embassy asked the Foreign Office to clarify whether the map was accurate or not, because if Britain had already taken up a position on the English Channel that was at odds with the Greek view on their rights in the Aegean, it would be illogical to ask British firms to refrain from exploring or drilling, on behalf of the Turks around the Greek islands. The answer of the Foreign Office was that no such agreement with the French over the Channel Islands had been reached but Britain would, in principle, favour an enclave solution where it could be shown that there was continuity (on grounds of the depth of the sea).[18]

Athens, on the other hand, approached the Anglo-French case in diametrically opposing ways and tried to convince the British that their interests were very similar in the sense that both governments adhered to the view that islands had their own continental shelf and should in any event be taken into account in any delimitation agreement. Greece also contemplated an extension of its territorial sea to twelve miles if it were not possible to negotiate with the Turks a satisfactory continental shelf delimitation agreement and give an assurance that the rights of *innocent passage* of the Turkish ships in the Greek territorial waters would be protected.[19]

Although the Cyprus Crisis in the summer of 1974 overshadowed the Greek–Turkish maritime dispute, it added another parameter to the confrontation over the Aegean. On the day of the Turkish military intervention in Cyprus in July 1974, Turkey started to challenge the hitherto existing and by the International Civil Aviation Organization approved Athens' air traffic control area[20] in the Aegean,[21] claiming that the Greek national airspace of 10 miles breadth (not recognised by Turkey and the rest of NATO) constituted a gross violation of international law. By having its military aircraft fly over the part of the area it disputed, which was responded to by Athens with interceptions of the Turkish aeroplanes, caused a precarious situation. Due to this, all foreign flights over the Aegean were grounded for six years, up to mid-1980, while the ongoing flights in question resulted in hazardous dogfights (Heraclides, 2010, pp. 81–82).

In a report by the CIA in August 1974 on this issue it is mentioned that the Turkish move to impose new air traffic regulations was a temporary problem related to the Cyprus Problem. However, the median line drawn by Turkey from the Greek–Turkish border in Thrace and from the Syrian–Turkish border was connected with some other claims as it encompassed the "disputed" Limnos island and increased the so-called dancer zone as it included the area involved in the dispute over oil.[22]

In December 1974, the hydrocarbons bonanza got a few cracks, as the principal exploration company, Oceanic, appeared to have difficulties marshalling the necessary money to go on to the next stage of exploitation. Apparently, it needed to find approximately $150 million to be able to begin commercial extraction in 1976. The company estimated that the area around Thassos could daily produce 50,000 barrels of crude oil, 10,000,000 cubic feet of natural gas and 1,000 tonnes of pure sulphur for at least 15 years. These represented Greece's total sulphur demand and approximately one-third of its crude oil requirements.[23] The total proven reserves, however, when the exploration started, turned out much more modest than expected (around 1,900 barrels per day).

In January 1975, Athens decided to make a proposal to Turkey for a joint recourse to the International Court of Justice over the outstanding delimitation of the continental shelf. The proposal was met positively by the Turkish government in Ankara that, however, formulated as a precondition that other issues such as the territorial waters, the delimitation of the continental shelf and the use of Aegean airspace should also be included in the agenda of the bilateral relations. By the end of May 1975, during the NATO summit in Brussels, the Greek Prime Minister Konstantinos Karamanlis and the Greek Foreign Minister Bitsios met with the US President Ford and the Secretary of State Kissinger to whom Karamanlis complained that the Turks were questioning the Aegean status quo that had existed since 1913 by claiming half of the Aegean Sea, including Greek territorial waters, seabed and airspace. Greece, so Karamanlis asserted, could renounce all of the Turkish claims but it decided to adopt a positive stance and accepted the joint recourse to the International Court of The Hague on the issue of the continental shelf but the Turks were not consenting to agreement (*compromis*) based on the international legality and the principle of resolving differences peacefully creating tensions that might lead to a war. President Ford replied that due to the Cyprus Crisis many problems within NATO and the US (as Congress decided to suspend US assistance to Turkey) had already been created but to exercise pressure on Ankara would be a wrong move, since the Turks were threatening to close down some very important US military bases in Turkey. It would be opportune to start talks. Kissinger on his part noted that some Turks were wishing a settlement but some did not. If Ecevit were Prime Minister, a solution would already have been found both in the Aegean and in Cyprus. Demirel, on the other hand, was afraid to show a conciliant attitude, because this could lead to a break-up of the government coalition (Konstantinos Karamanlis Archeio, 2005, vol. 8, pp. 415–423)

In these days, the Foreign Ministers of the two countries came together to prepare the soil for the meeting of the Prime Ministers. The Joint Communiqué of the ministers' meeting announced that talks on the continental shelf and other bilateral issues on the level of experts would be soon assumed. and a new meeting between the ministers at the end of the month. A few days later the long-expected meeting between Karamanlis and Demirel took place. Demirel laid out all issues which, in his opinion, should be negotiated on, the Cyprus Problem, the FIR issue, the continental shelf and the militarisation of the Aegean islands. Karamanlis retorted that the FIR problem was caused by Turkey's arbitrary deeds but he had no objection to the two parties putting together a committee of experts, thereby seeking a mutually beneficial solution to all outstanding problems. With regard to the military status of the islands, Karamanlis had the opinion that the issue had a legal and a practical aspect. Turkey should not invoke the *Paris Treaty* [24] because it had not signed it, while the *Montreux Treaty* had annulled the demilitarisation of Lemnos and some other islands. Greece according to Karamanlis, had resorted to fortification for purely defensive reasons out of fear of a possible Turkish attack, as it had been the case in 1974. If the other issues were resolved, this issue would be resolved on its own because there would be no need for Greece to maintain an army there. He urged Turkey to sign the agreement for a joint recourse[25] to the International Court of The Hague (Konstantinos Karamanlis Archive, 2005, pp. 96–98 and 420–423).

In September 1975, and after strong pressure from the opposition, the Demirel government announced the postponement of the experts' meeting in Paris on the grounds that the Greek side was insisting on the *compromis*. The truth is that the Greek side attached great importance to this matter for two reasons: it did not believe a solution to the dispute would be possible through bilateral negotiations, whereas a legal decision, imposed by an international, independent body, even not favourable for Greece, would stand a better chance to be accepted by the Greek public (Valinakis, 1989, pp. 210–214).

Domestic politics played a significant role in both countries. Andreas Papandreou, the new increasingly popular charismatic leader of the socialist opposition in Greece, was accusing Prime Minister Karamanlis of "losing the psychological war" with Turkey. In Turkey, after receiving harsh domestic criticism in Ankara for agreeing to the recourse to the International Court of Justice, Demirel gradually withdrew from this commitment. Demirel was attacked by the head of the opposition, Ecevit, for allowing the balance of power in the Aegean to change against Turkey. Deputy Prime Minister of Turkey's far-right party, Turkes, even increased the stakes by declaring that the islands "near the Turkish shores, especially the Dodecanese, must belong to Turkey" (Katsoulas, 2022, p. 161).

Thus, despite the agreement to continue the dialogue on Aegean issues, already in the first months of 1976, the climate between the two countries deteriorated. At the end of January 1976, the first meeting of experts took place with Ambassador Bilge and the Director of Political Affairs Ioannis Tzounis, which Greek diplomat Kosmadopoulos described as a recitation of monologues after the Greek representative insisted on an appeal to the International Court of Justice and the Turkish one raised the idea of co-exploitation. Moreover, amid the toxic domestic political climate, the known Turkish nationalist Ecevit, accused the government of letting Greece tip the balance in the Aegean to the detriment of Turkey. Demirel could not appear as the politician who would lose the benefits secured under Ecevit; the political cost was high. Therefore, under enormous political pressure, as it was the case with joint recourse to the International Court, the unstable four-party Turkish government embarked upon the resumption of surveys in the

Aegean by the oceanographic research ship Hora (later renamed Sizmik-1) torpedoing the talks. The ship entered the area between Lemnos and Lesvos, considered high sea for Turkey, but not for Greece, while Ankara sent a strongly worded Note warning Athens of the consequences should Greece attack on an unarmed ship whose mission was purely scientific. Once again Greek–Turkish relations came to the brink of war. Four days later, the Turkish ship returned to the harbour on the Turkish mainland where it had sailed off and a few hours later Athens decided to appeal simultaneously to the UN Security Council and the International Court of Justice of The Hague. Ecevit accused Karamanlis of deliberately asking for the *compromis* so that Greece could expand its territorial waters and appropriate the entire Aegean Sea and its continental shelf (Rizas, 2009).

To the dismay of Athens, the UN Security Council avoided condemning Turkey for its actions, calling instead the governments of Greece and Turkey to resume direct negotiations over their differences. It further appealed to them to do everything within their power to ensure that these result in mutually acceptable solutions. It also invited both sides to continue to take into account "all appropriate judicial means, in particular the International Court of Justice", for the settlement of any remaining legal differences in connection with their present dispute (International Court of Justice, 1976, p. 1235).

The statement favoured Turkey by the reference to negotiations and the lack of any condemnation for Turkish actions in the Aegean as Greece had pursued, and Greece by avoiding any reference to the demilitarisation of the eastern Aegean islands as Turkey had pursued and made a reference to the International Court of Justice (Valinakis, 1989, pp. 210–214).

Although many scholars have pinpointed the ambiguity of the resolution's wording, the overall handling of the issue by the Security Council took some steam out of the dispute (Bahcheli, 1990, p. 135).

The dispute was defused by another development as well. In November 1976, the Greek government passed Law 468/1976 on the exploration, exploration and exploitation of hydrocarbons and commissioned the French Petroleum Institute to conduct a survey in the Aegean Sea. After the perusal of the research data that had been gathered by the Americans during the military junta, the French company pinpointed as the area of greatest interest the Bambouras area, 10 miles east of the island Thassos and beyond the 6 miles of Greece's territorial waters (Kathimerini, 2022).

In the same year, the Greek state proceeded with a unilateral recourse to the International Court of Justice that, however, is known for its reluctance to accept unilateral appeals (Roukounas, 2008, pp. 331–337). More precisely, as it can be inferred from the proceedings of the case published by the International Court of Justice, Greece asked the Court to declare that the Greek islands in the area were entitled to their lawful portion of the continental shelf and to delimit the respective parts of that shelf appertaining to Greece and Turkey. At the same time, it requested provisional measures indicating that, pending the Court's judgment, neither state should, without the other's consent, engage in exploration or research with respect to the shelf in question. The government of Turkey did not file any pleadings and it was not represented at the oral proceedings. However, the attitude of the Government of Turkey with regard to the question of the Court's jurisdiction was defined in its separate communications to the Court.

In May 1976, the Greek Foreign Minister Bitsios briefed his West German counterpart in Oslo on the stand of the Greek–Turkish relationship. According to the Greek Foreign Minister, the Greek public opinion was ready to accept the decision of the Court but ruled out any discussion on joint ventures in the Aegean Sea as long as there was no agreement on the maritime boundaries.[26]

Concurrently, Washington was very sceptical about Greece's recourse to the International Court of The Hague, supporting direct negotiations. This was conveyed to Karamanlis by Jimmy Carter himself when Karamnlis travelled to Washington to inform the Americans about Greece's undertaking. Karamanlis also agreed that there was no doubt that it is best to have direct contact and negotiations. But if there are no results, then that is why we have international institutions and Courts. Demirel consented to this solution but for internal political reasons backed off. The same happened with Greece's proposition to sign a non-aggression and arms control pact. The Turks initially consented to the signing of such a pact but later pulled back, perhaps for domestic political reasons. Demirel himself asked Karamanlis not to reveal the initial consent, since that would create unsurmountable problems domestically and blow up the whole negotiation process. Therefore, so Karamanlis said to the Americans, Greece could not sustain a dialogue under such circumstances.[27]

On 11 September 1976, the Court found that the indication of such measures was not required and, as Turkey had denied the Court's competence, ordered that the proceedings should first concern the question of jurisdiction. In a second judgment delivered on 19 December 1978, the Court found that jurisdiction to deal with the case was not conferred upon it by either of the two instruments relied upon by Greece. The first was the application of the General Act for Pacific Settlement of International Disputes of 1928 which was not accepted by the Court due to Greece's reservation upon its accession to the act. The second was the Joint Communiqué of 31 May 1975 (resulting from the Karamanlis–Demirel meeting in Brussels) and to the context in which it was agreed and issued. The Court concluded that the Joint Communiqué was not intended to, and did not, constitute an immediate commitment by the Greek and Turkish Prime Ministers, on behalf of their respective governments, to accept unconditionally the unilateral submission of the dispute to the Court. Moreover, in the Court's opinion, the Brussels Communiqué did not furnish a valid basis for establishing the Court's jurisdiction to entertain the application filed by Greece on 10 August 1976 (The International Court of Justice, 1978).

Although this decision might be regarded as a setback for Greece, in fact, the International Court was unable after nearly two and one-half years of deliberating on procedural questions to rule over the substantive issues of continental shelf delimitation indicating the complexity of the matter (Bahcheli, 1990, p. 137).

Besides the Court's decision, various meetings between the Prime Ministers as well as the Secretaries-General of the Foreign Ministries of Greece and Turkey took place in the next but to no avail. The positions of the two sides had been crystalised (and in fact remained more or less unchanged ever since) on the following points that in the course of time became a sanctuary for both sides: Greece referred to the 1958 Geneva Convention of the Law of the Sea that grants the islands their own territorial sea and continental shelf, whereas Turkey advocated the supremacy of the jurisdictional right of continental land masses over those of the islands, supporting factually a median line between the Greek and Turkish mainland completely disregarding the islands. Greece claimed that every point of the median line should be equidistant from the nearest point of the baselines formed by the eastern Aegean Greek islands and the Turkish coasts provided that special circumstances do not justify another boundary. In the Greek view, the islands did not constitute special circumstances because of their number, size, population and economic life. Further, the right of Greece to explore and exploit the natural resources of the Aegean islands is exclusive, a fact which, in the Greek view, was recognised by the Geneva Convention and the International Court of Justice. Therefore, Turkey did not have the right to undertake these activities, despite the fact that Greece did not explore or exploit these natural resources. Turkey, on the other hand, claimed that the median line/

equidistance principle was not part of customary international law. Even within Article 6, the median line/equidistance was considered as being subsidiary to the primary obligation to effect delimitation by agreement. Furthermore, according to the Turkish argumentation, the second requirement was that no special circumstances existed in the delimitation area, a view, which had been confirmed in the North Sea cases of 1960 where the median line/equidistance was regarded not as the sole method of delimitation, but simply as one method among others. Furthermore, Turkey also blamed Greece for the US arms embargo on Turkey which Greece disclaimed on the grounds that this was beyond the Greek government's power and did not control the Congress and the Greek lobby in the US either. For a short time, Athens appeared ready to negotiate – except the continental shelf that Greece regards as the only outstanding issue to be solved by an International Court – on the airspace control over the Aegean as well, although the Greek view was that this was not an exercise of sovereign rights but only a matter of technical responsibility (Konstantinos Karamanlis Archive, 2005, vol. 10, pp. 273–274 and 326–329).

Ahead of the Turkish general elections in June 1977, there was a widespread fear that the confrontation might worsen. After its exclusion from the US arms aid programme due to the arms embargo, Turkey voiced bitterness towards the Americans, complaining that Greece, particularly the Greek air force, was about to gain superiority in the Aegean. So, the CIA gauged that due to its dependency on the US arms supply, Turkey would be reluctant to attack Greece and risk forfeiting the substantial arms aid it still received from the United States. Thus, there was no convincing evidence that Turkey was seriously considering any sort of aggressive military action to defend or further its Aegean interests despite the impasse at the negotiating table. Ultimately, according to the CIA, "a peaceful resolution of the dispute would depend on the Greek's willingness to accept a significant role for Turkey and Turkey's willingness to settle for substantially less than the equal rights they seemed intent on securing".[28]

During a summit that took place in Montreux in 1978 between Karamanlis and Ecevit, it was agreed that bilateral talks between the Secretaries-General of both foreign ministries would continue. It was an attempt to maintain open lines of direct communication, at a senior level, always it was clear that the views of Ankara and Athens diverged on all issues. Over a span of three years, several meetings between Byron Theodoropoulos for Greece and diplomats (initially Sukru Elekdag) for Turkey, took place either in Ankara or in Athens on three pressing issues: the signing of a non-aggression pact or a friendship treaty; the delimitation of the continental shelf and on the air traffic control zones without any results. It seems that for the Greek side, the central Aegean issue was security, while for the Turkish side, the main issue was access to the Aegean seabed. In the State Department's assessment, from the Greek perspective, the Aegean competition was not limited to seabed rights. There also was a deeply rooted suspicion of Turkish intentions which rendered international negotiations over seabed rights, the airspace issue difficult, a vital security question and a potentially inflammatory domestic issue. Virtually all Greeks accepted the worst-case view of a nation against which their ancestors repeatedly fought to gain independence and therefore the Turkish claim on the seabed was the first slice in an expansionist Turkey's salami tactic, designed to cut Greek islands, and even parts of Thrace, out from Greek sovereignty. The State Department also believed that Karamanlis had the authority to impose his wishes, including a wish for a peaceful settlement, on his hard-line civilian and military advisers, the bureaucrats who support them as well as to sell any reasonable settlement to the public, despite the inevitable nationalistic demagoguery of Papandreou.[29]

Thus, the two sides which at the same time were consumed by the securing of advantages in the context of Greece's re-integration into NATO, remained unflinching in their basic positions. responsibility in managing it. Unsurprisingly, the Greek Socialist political leader Andreas Papandreou cancelled them unilaterally when he came to power in October 1981.

Another aspect of the Greek–Turkish maritime dispute, which came to the fore in the 1970s and has been haunting the Greek–Turkish relationship to date, was the military status of the eastern Aegean islands (Limnos, Samothrace, Mytilene, Chios, Samos and Ikaria and the Dodecanese islands). The militarisation of these islands had been initiated in the 1960s, and was however accelerated by the Karamanlis government in the 1970s as a response to the Turkish invasion of Cyprus.[30]

In May 1972, before the events in Cyprus in the summer of 1974, when the issue of the militarisation of the island Lemnos first arose, the Research Department of the Southern European Section of the Foreign Office prepared a report about the military status of the eastern Aegean islands. According to the report Mytilene, Chios, Samos and Ikaria as well as those islands ceded by Italy to Greece by the *Treaty of Paris* 1947 (Agathonisi, Astypalaia, Chalki, Kalymnos, Karpathos, Kasos, Kastellorizo, Kos, Lipsi, Leros, Nisyros, Patmos, Rhodes) were to be demilitarised, and nothing has occurred subsequently to alter this treaty agreement. There was, however, confusion about the wording of the protocol at the end of the Montreux Convention which states that Turkey may immediately remilitarise the zone of the Straits as defined in the Preamble to the said Convention also affecting Lemnos and Somothraki.[31]

In contrast to the Turkish accusations on the military status of the islands, Greece retorted by invoking the danger emanating from the Aegean Army headquartered in Izmir and deployed along Turkey's Aegean coast, opposite the Greek eastern Aegean islands. The Aegean Army was organised in the mid-1970s following the Turkish invasion of Cyprus and has been ever since a controversial issue in Greek–Turkish bilateral relations. Greeks believe that the army with its large amphibious landing fleet directly threatens Cyprus and the Greek islands, while Turks claim the Aegean Army comprises only training forces. In the 1980s, Turkish officials, however, justified maintaining the army in the event they needed to provide rapid reinforcement to north Cyprus. The CIA also shared this opinion at the same timespan estimating that the Aegean army was a training establishment and likely a headquarters for Turkish forces in Cyprus, providing fresh troops and equipment for rotation to north Cyprus.[32]

Notes

1 PRO: FCO 9/2009: "Telegram from the British Embassy in Athens to Energy Department Foreign & Commonwealth Office 1 March 1974".
2 PRO: FCO 9/2009: "Telegram from the British Embassy in Athens to the British embassy in Ankara 11 February 1974".
3 It is about the so-called Nord Sea Cases examining among other islands' effect on the demarcation line, which, together with the configuration of the coast and the length of the coastline, is presumably the quintessence of the Greek–Turkish maritime dispute.
4 PRO: FCO 9/2009: "Telegrams from the British Embassy in Athens to the Foreign Office April 1974".
5 The *Third Conference on the Law of the Sea*, negotiated between 1973 and 1982 was a milestone in the maritime law and is commonly accepted as one of the greatest achievements of the United Nations since its creation and as the universal legal text governing the seas. Greece and Turkey participated in the negotiations carried out under the auspices of the United Nations. Among others, the Turkish delegation submitted proposals aimed at attaining an exception to the Aegean Sea to 12-mile rule but not questioning the rule in general. The main trends at the Conference and the package deal approach were not favourable to the position of Turkey. Turkey also made several attempts to limit the marine spaces of islands. Its proposals were met with strong objections from states with islands. Greek delegation's efforts to form the archipelagic regime so as to

be applied to the Aegean Sea, which would appertain Greece sovereignty over an even greater proportion of the Aegean, did not come to fruition either. The conference's definition of archipelagos was that states consist entirely of islands (Stergiou, 2022, pp. 22–26). Against this background, the *Third Conference on the Law of the Sea* became a field of contention. In order to promote their cause, both countries were endeavoured to elicit other countries' support. For example, in March 1976 the Greek Ambassador in Bonn visited the Federal German Foreign Ministry to draw the attention of the Germans to the Turkish proposals (Definition of the Aegean Sea as half-closed, introduction of the notion "Equity" as method of delimitation of maritime zones et al). German Federal Archive, Political Archive of the German Foreign Ministry: Folder 110223, "Visit of the Greek Ambassador Frydas to D 2 Bonn 17 March 1976".

6 PRO: FCO 9/2009: "B. Hitch's Report of the Continental Shelf in the Aegean Sea, 15 March 1974".

7 PRO: FCO 9/2010: "Telegrams from the British Embassy in Ankara to the European Department of the Foreign & Commonwealth Office, June 1974".

8 PRO: FCO 9/2009: "Internal Report of the Foreign Office on the Greek/ Turkish Border in the Aegean 26 March 1974".

9 PRO: FCO 9/2009: "Telegram from the British Embassy in Ankara to the Foreign Office, 5 March 1974, subject: Turkish reactions: Aegean Oil"; "Telegrams from the British Embassy in Ankara and in Athens to the Foreign Office, March and April 1974"; "Telegram from the British Embassy in Ankara to the Foreign Office and the British embassy in Athens 26 February 1974, subject the Aegean and oil".

10 PRO: FCO 9/2009: "Telegram from the British Embassy in Athens to the Foreign Office (Southern European Department), 16 January 1974".

11 As the British noted the Greek minority living in Istanbul declined from over 100,000 Greeks after the Lausanne settlement to about 15,000 (Greek estimate) in June 1974. The community periodically suffered harassment and there was continuing evidence that they were under some pressure to leave, though during the Cyprus Crisis there appears to have been very little activity against the minority despite allegations to the contrary. The Ecumenical Patriarch, resident in Istanbul, was reported to be disturbed at the continuing loss of his flock, but he would certainly not leave Istanbul unless expelled by force. The Turks would be glad to see the end of the Greek Church in Istanbul, but they were aware that if they were to expel the Patriarch there might be repercussions for the Turks in Western Thrace. Additionally, any attempt to remove or abolish the Patriarchate could lead to international pressures, notably from the United States, because the Soviet Union would probably foster moves for the Patriarch of Moscow to assume the Primacy of the Orthodox Church. Concerning the "Turkish community in Greece", the British observed that it had increased slightly since Lausanne and at the time numbered about 120,000. In 1964, the Turkish population on the Dodecanese Islands of Rhodes and Kos was around 5,000. In Thrace they had long been subjected to petty persecution. Following the Cyprus Crisis, the Turkish Embassy in Athens alleged that, though there had been some improvements for the Moslem minority, their conditions overall had worsened considerably. Many

members of the community had reached the conclusion that they would sooner or later have to leave Greece for Turkey. The difficulty did not arise from high-level policy but from the way in which, at local village or police level, administrative rules could be used to persecute the Moslems and from local brutality. The British embassy in Athens considered this assessment to be accurate. PRO: FCO 9/2012: Report of the South-East European Department on Greco-Turkish relations: a "global approach", 31 Oktober 1974.

12 PRO: FCO 9/2009: "Telegram from the British Embassy in Athens to the Foreign Office, 2 April 1974".

13 CIA releases 2017: "Telegram from the US Embassy in Greece to the CIA Headquarters 30 May 1974. Subject: Greece-Turkey Aegean Dispute".

14 PRO: FCO 9/2010: "Telegram from the British Embassy in Ankara to the Foreign Office (Southern European Department), 31 May 1974, subject: Greek/Turkish dispute in the Aegean".

15 PRO: FCO 9/2010: "Telegrams from the British Embassy in Athens to the Foreign Office and Report of A. C. Goodison of the Southern European Department of the Foreign Office on Aegean, June 1974".

16 PRO: FCO 9/2010: "Telegram from the British Embassy in Athens to the Foreign Office, 5 June 1974".

17 CIA releases 2017: "CIA Warning Notice to the White House 7 June 1974, subject: The Greek-Turkish Aegean Dispute".

18 PRO: FCO 9/2011: "Telegram from the British embassy in Ankara to the Foreign Office and vice versa 7 June 1974".

19 PRO: FCO 9/2012: "Hitch's Report on the Conversation About Continental Shelf Delimitations between the Greek Ambassador in London and Vincel Evans and Hitch, 4 December 1974"; "Evans' Report on a Conversation with the Greek Ambassador, Rousos 5 November 1974".

20 The delimitation of national airspace claimed by Greece is unique as it does not coincide with the boundary of the territorial waters. Pursuant to the Decree of 6 September 1931 in conjunction with the Law 5017/1931 it extends to 10 nautical miles.

21 Athens Civil Flight Information Region, sometimes extended in places very close to the Turkish coast.

22 CIA releases 2017: "Report dated 9 August 1974, Subject: Turkish Intentions in the Aegean".

23 PRO: FCO 9/2012: "Telegram from the British Embassy in Athens to the Foreign Office, 11 December 1974".

24 With the *Paris Peace Treaty* of 10 February 1947 Italy ceded sovereignty of the Dodecanese islands to Greece.

25 The International Court in the Hague can only hear cases involving states that have accepted its jurisdiction, either by making an agreement (compromise) to submit the specific dispute to the Court or by ratifying a treaty which specifies that disputes under the treaty will be submitted to the Court and its jurisdiction is compulsory.

26 German Federal Archive, Political Archive of the German Federal Foreign Ministry: Folder 110223, "Meeting between the Greek and the West German Foreign Minister in Oslo on 21 May 1976".

27 FRUS 1977–1980, volume XXI, Cyprus; Turkey; Greece, Document no. 166, "Memorandum of Conversation between the US President Jimmy

Carter, the US Secretary of State Cyrus Vance, Dr Zbigniew Brzezinski, the Assistant to the President for National Security Affairs Clark Clifford and Robert Hunter, Staff Member, National Security Council (Notetaker) and Greek Prime Minister Konstantinos Karamanlis, Greek Foreign Minister Dimitris Bitsios and Petros Molyviatis, Director General of the Prime Minister's Political Cabinet, in London on 10 May 1977".

28 CIA releases 2017: "Memorandum for the Director of Central Intelligence from the Assistant National Intelligence Officer for Western Europe, Subject: Turkish Aegean Intentions, 19 May 1977".

29 Wikileaks: "Foreign Relations: Greece-Turkey: prospects for Agreement or Conflict in the Aegean. Cable from the Department of State to the Commander in Chief European Command in Vaihingen Germany 22 March 1979". https://wikileaks.org/plusd/cables/1979STATE071262_e.html; US Department of State releases 2014: "Telegram from the US Embassy in Athens to the Secretary of State and US embassies, subject: Karamanlis' mood, 30 June 1978".

30 On the arguments of both sides around the militarisation of the eastern Aegean islands see Stergiou, 2022, pp. 14–17).

31 PRO: FCO 9/2011: "Report of the Research Department of the Foreign Office on the Aegean Islands, May 1972"; "Brooke Turner's Report on his Conversation with Diamantopoulos, the Counsellor at the Greek embassy in Landon on the Militarisation of Lemnos, October 1972".

32 CIA releases 2017: "The Greek-Turkish Dispute: Effects on NATO. A Defence Research Report. Defence Intelligence Agency November 1986".

33 The 2005 edition was made by *Kathimerini* newspaper and is divided in more volumes than the 1997 one.

References

Primary Sources

CIA Releases 2017

Foreign Relations of the United States (FRUS), 1977–1980. Volume XXI, Cyprus; Turkey; Greece (cited as FRUS)

German Federal Archive, Political Archive of the German Federal Foreign Ministry

Public Record Office (PRO)

US Department of State Releases

Wikileaks

NATO Archive

Secondary sources

Bahcheli, T., 1990. *Greek-Turkish Relations since 1955*. New York: Avalon Publishing.

Hale, W., 2013. *Turkish foreign policy since 1774* (3rd ed.). London/New York: Routledge.

Heraclides, A., 2010. *The Greek-Turkish Conflict in the Aegean. Imagined Enemies*. New York: Palgrave.

International Court of Justice1978. Aegean Sea Continental Shelf (Greece v. Turkey). www.icj-cij.org/en/case/62

International Court of Justice1976. International legal materials 1976. *American Society of International Law* 15(5), Resolution 395, 25 August 1976.

Kathimerini Newspaper, 7 December 2022. www.kathimerini.gr/politics/for eign-policy/562168309/ellinotoyrkika-i-odysseia-ton-ydrogonanthrakon/

Katsoulas, S., 2022. *The United States and Greek-Turkish Relations. The Guardian's Dilemma*. London and New York: Routledge.

Konstantinos Karamanlis Archeio. Gegonota kai Keimena (1997 and 2005)[33] [Konstantinos Karamanlis Archive. Incidents and Texts], volumes 8 and 10. Athens: Idryma K. Karamanlis-Ekdotiki Athinon Publisher.

Lie, Ø., Fürstenau, J., Bellas S., & Tsifoutidis, G., 2014. A Fresh Look at the Oil and Gas Potential of Greece. *Geo EXPRO*, 10(6). www.geoexpro.com/a rticles/2014/03/a-fresh-look-at-the-oil-and-gas-potential-of-greece

Papachelas, ⬚., 2021. *Ena Skoteino Domatio 1967-1974 [A Dark Room 1967–1974]*. Athens: Metechmio Publisher.

Rizas, S., 2008. Atlanticism and Europeanism in Greek foreign and security policy in the 1970s, *Southeast European and Black Sea Studies*, 8 (1), 51–66.

Rizas, S., 2009. Managing a conflict between allies: United States policy towards Greece and Turkey in relation to the Aegean dispute, 1974–1976. *Cold War History*, 9 (3), 367–387.

Roukounas, E., 2008. *O Konstantinos Karamanlis kai I eiriniki epilysi ton diethnon diaforon: I prosfigi tiw Elladas sto Diethnes Dikastirio tis Hagis [Konstaninos Karamanlis and the peaceful settlement of international disputes: Greece's appeal to the International Court of Justice in Hague]*. In K. Svolopoulos, K. Botsiou & E. Hatzivasiliou (eds.), *O Konstantinos Karamanlis ston Eikosto Aiona* [Konstantinos Karamanlis in the Twentieth Century]. Conference ProceedingsVol. II (pp. 331–337). Athens: Konstantinos Karamanlis Foundation.

Stergiou, A., 2022. *The Greek-Turkish Maritime Dispute. Resisting the Future*. Switzerland AG: Springer Nature.

Syrigos, A., 2016. *Oi Ellinotourkikes 1967–1974. Apo tin Synantisi ston Evro stin Eisvoli stin Kypro [The Greek–Turkish Relations 1967–1974. From the Encounter in Evros to the Invasion in Cyprus]*. In the Hellenic Parliament Foundation (ed.), *I Dictatoria ton Syntamatarchon kai I Apokatastasi tis Dimocratias* [The Colonels dictatorship and the restore of Parliamentarism]. Conference Proceedings (pp. 313–336). Athens: The Hellenic Parliament Foundation.

The International Court of Justice, 1978. Reports of Judgments, Advisory Opinions and Orders. Aegean Sea, Continental Shelf Case (Greece v. Turkey) Judgment of 19 December 1978.

Tsitselikis, K., 2006. I Amoiveotita os oros efarmogis ton ypochreosevn Elladas kai Tourkias apenantistis meionotites tous [The Reciprocity as a rule in the obligations of Greece and Turkey towards their minorities]. In University of West Macedonia (ed.), *Aspects of Transition and the European Perspective of the Balkan Countries* (pp. 865–878). Florina: Conference Proceedings.

Valinakis, G., 1989. *Eisagogi stin Elliniki Exoteriki Politiki 1949–1988* [*Introduction into the Greek Foreign Policy 1949–1988*]. Thessaloniki: Paratiritis Publisher.

United Nations Convention on the Law of the Sea: www.un.org/depts/los/convention_agreements/texts/unclos/unclos_e.pdf

Zafiropoulos, G., (2012). *Exploration History and Hydrocarbon Potential of Greece*. Institute of Energy for South-East Europe (ed.), Proceedings of the Workshop on Hydrocarbons in Greece, 26–27 April 2012. www.iene.gr/workshop-for-hydrocarbon/articlefiles/session4/zafiropoulos.pdf

Internet Sources

www.turkishgreek.org/kuetuephane/item/50-bern-agreement-between-turkey-and-greece-11-november-1976

3 Greece's reintegration into NATO

Greece's withdrawal from the NATO military structure was not only a reaction to the alliance's inertia in the summer of 1974. It also was a concession to the public anti-American sentiment about the US relationship with the colonels and the generally perceived US role in the Cyprus Crisis. A string of US moves towards the Junta such as the resumption of arms shipments to Greece after a three-year embargo, US Vice President Spiros Agnew's official visit to Greece, as well as the signing of a military agreement between the United States and Greece, were perceived as signs of vivid US support to the colonels (Papadimitriou, 2007, p. 409). Furthermore, US support to Turkey because of its tremendous geostrategic value to NATO and Western security interests, although there is no evidence of US interventionism of high intensity, enabled the rise of strong anti-American sentiments among the Greek Cypriots as well (Kontos, 2016, p. 45).

Therefore, already in August 1974, the US Ambassador made his suggestions to the Secretary of State in Washington vis-a-vis the improvement of the image of the United States in Greece. More precisely, he proposed that once Turkish–Greek relations quieted down, the US should make every effort to a) be as forthcoming as possible in the Greek programme to modernise its armed forces, since the Greek military from the lowest to the highest ranks still preferred American equipment over that of the other allies, although sometimes delivery schedules and economics had forced the Greeks otherwise; b) provide some assistance in obtaining credit to carry Greece over the difficult balance of payments position; c) with the exception of providing assistance to Greece to modernise its army, encourage NATO allies similarly to act along the foregoing lines; d) since Greece was deeply offended that NATO Secretary General Luns had refused to postpone his vacation during the Cyprus Crisis to be more active at the NATO Council meetings regarding the Greek–Turkish conflict, thereby taking

DOI: 10.4324/9781003350033-4

some steps to repair this "feeling of wounded *philotimo* (sense of self-esteem)".[1]

Other leaders of NATO countries showed in private conversations an understanding of Athens' actions and its decision to pull out from the alliance due to NATO indifference at the crucial moment despite the legal restrictions a NATO intervention was faced with. However, no one was ready to terminate its defence cooperation with Turkey.[2]

As of the autumn of 1974, the Athens–Ankara–NATO relationship ushered into a new era. Greece had stopped taking part in the NATO Defence Planning Committee, in joint military drills and sharing information with its previous allies on the common air defence. It also decided to single itself out from the Defence Review Committee, another body of the political structure of the alliance. However, it continued participating in some activities of the political structure of the alliance, which Athens believed were not related to its withdrawal declaration in August 1974 with a view of averting the making of harmful decisions for Greece.[3]

As the US government officially admitted, given the miliary base rights restrictions imposed by the Karamanlis government, Greece was, contrary to Turkey, of marginal importance to US security interests in the Middle East. US military influence in the Middle East (present and potential) would suffer substantially if Turkey were to turn its back on the United States. On the other hand, Greece's withdrawal from NATO undermined the cohesion of the alliance on its south-eastern flank, as it did the US embargo on arms sales to Turkey (Congressional Research Service Library of Congress, 1975, p. 18).

The Greek case should not be compared with the French case some years ago, although Karamanlis must have been influenced by the French detachment from NATO in the 1960s, while he was in Paris. The fact that Greece remained in the political structure of NATO had barely symbolic meaning and did not commit any of both sides to provide support to each other in the event of war. France, on the contrary, after its withdrawal, had declared that, in the case of war, it would participate in the alliance activities. Moreover, France was a nuclear power, had its own weapons production industry, did not confront the hostile attitude of a NATO member state like Greece did, and, finally, did not border on any Warsaw Pact country. The only thing remaining in favour of Greek security was older NATO operational plans engulfing Greece as a frontline state. Greece's defence leadership estimated or hoped that, given the US military presence in Greece since the 1950s, it was not opportune strategically and operationally for the alliance to change them despite Greece's withdrawal.[4]

In September 1974, Kissinger authorised with a priority message the US mission to NATO to work closely with Luns to work out the new relationship between NATO and Greece by saying that the content and tactics of any negotiations with Athens are of particular importance to each individual ally and especially to the US because of its bilateral military relationship with Greece.[5]

The Greek military leadership was, also, convinced at the time that this kind of limited cooperation with NATO in certain areas of defence such as planning and nuclear support was very opportune for Greek security. On the one hand, it committed the alliance to provide assistance in case of an attack from the northern Communist neighbours, on the other hand, this arrangement relieved Greece of its obligation to contribute forces, to put under NATO control the military capabilities and to participate in military drillings. It was uncertain, however, whether and to what degree NATO would get involved in a regional war in Balkan. Although the withdrawal was still necessary as long as there was no guarantee against the Turkish threat, in peace times, the country was deprived of many benefits linked to participation in the alliance: keeping up with the technological developments at the level of defence; the financing of infrastructure projects, the ability to prevent within the alliance what benefited Turkey and harmed Greece; maintaining the interest of the international war industry to participate in procurements of the Greek state, etc.[6]

Against this background, some US diplomats suggested not to exclude Greece from infrastructure projects, except Greece decided to suspend its participation in them on its own or stopped employing infrastructure-financed facilities to the benefit of NATO.[7] In this respect, Washington hoped that Karamanlis, an experienced and pragmatic statesman, could keep Greece, if not within the immediate sphere of US influence, at least within the Western world (Klapsis, 2011, pp. 67–68).

In fact, the Karamanlis government continued to accommodate some American interests in the region in the following years as well. In February 1978, the Greek Minister of Defense Averof appeared in parliament to answer several queries on military facility topics and the existence of nuclear weapons in Greece submitted by deputies of the fierce anti-American opposition socialist party and outspoken critics of the US military presence in Greece. Averof stated that he could neither confirm nor deny the presence of nuclear weapons in Greece, adding that Greek control of American bases was almost complete, would further improve in the immediate future and that the American facilities "served many interests, but there are none which did not serve Greek interests".[8]

On the other side, Turkey also had a difficult relationship with NATO because it felt unequally treated in Cyprus and in the Aegean especially after the US Congress imposed the arms three-year embargo (1975–1978) because of the Turkish invasion of Cyprus. In the 1970s and 1980s, all the US administrations were motivated by a desire to strengthen the Turkish army, the largest standing army in NATO after the Americans, and to compensate Turkey for the material losses suffered during the arms three-year embargo. The Aegean balance of power, as important as it was for Greece, was a distinctly secondary consideration. Unlike Greece, which was considered difficult, Turkey was considered to be alliance-minded (Stergiou, 2021, pp. 180–181).

Given Greece's strong post-war attachment to the West, the State Department and other NATO allies regarded Greece's withdrawal from NATO as temporary and rather a protest act that would not be followed up. Therefore, the alliance showed no particular interest in starting negotiations for the withdrawal. Washinton preferred instead, as it is literally mentioned in the archival documents, to let Greece take the initiative on steps in the direction of further withdrawal, put no pressure whatsoever on Athens to formalise further its evolving relationship with NATO, urge Secretary General Luns and other permanent representatives to NATO to limit probing of Greeks on their new relationship with NATO. In a strange way, for the allies it was an open question whether Greece was still contributing forces to the integrated command since Greek officers remained at military headquarters despite the official withdrawal, with the exception of Izmir. However, the Greek military representatives still working in NATO did not receive documents dealing with Greece–NATO and Greece–Turkey issues and did not participate in discussions around those documents. Furthermore, despite the *de facto* steps Greece had taken regarding its participation in alliance military activities, the contractual basis for Greek participation remained as it existed before August 1974. Therefore, Luns continued to believe the alliance should not take the initiative to change the Greek–NATO relationship. The completion of the withdrawal, thus, was for months in abeyance, as the Greek side wanted first to clarify some outstanding bilateral issues with the United States and later proceed into negotiations with the alliance. Only, after the Americans signalled that the two issues were intertwined, did Athens complete the withdrawal.[9]

Not being under the NATO umbrella, the Karamanlis government proceeded with a reorganisation of the Greek army by building up defence capabilities, re-equipping the armed forces, strengthening defence infrastructure and fostering a sense of professionalism within the officer corps. It was obvious that the "threat from the East", as the perceived Turkish threat was called, posed Greece new defence challenges. Defence expenditures, mainly aimed at acquiring French and American weapons, increased in real terms from around $3.8 billion in 1973 to $7 billion by 1977. At the same time, the government undertook the first steps towards developing a domestic arms industry. For this reason, on 11 September 1974, the Greek government signed a joint letter of intent with Lockheed Aircraft Corporation establishing a multilevel cooperation. In 1977, the Greek Parliament passed a bill (Act 660) restructuring the armed services.[10]

In 1975, Ankara instituted a five-year national plan, the so-called *1975–1980 Force Goals*, aimed at increasing the national defence capabilities and, given Greece's absence, Turkey's overall defence posture in NATO's southern flank. The initial planning earmarked the allocation of 53.5 billion Turkish liras for modernisation programmes of the Armed Forces. The US arms embargo derailed, however, the plan at its initial stage.[11]

Comparatively, Greece allocated during this period an average of 6% of GDP to defence uses yearly. Turkey's defence spending was 4.7 % of GDP yearly. The NATO average for the same period was 3.3% (excluding Turkey and Greece). As a result, both countries regularly ranked as the NATO members with the highest defence burden. The size of their armed forces followed a different pattern compared to defence spending. Greece's armed forces declined from an all time high of 200,000 in 1977 to an average of about 105,000 until the early 1990s. Turkey's armed forces on the other hand, despite the yearly fluctuations, followed an upward path throughout the post-1974 period. Different population growth rates between Turkey and Greece might well explain this (Kollias, 1995, pp. 141–142).

In October 1975, in a turnaround, Athens announced that it would consider rejoining NATO military command, after its bold leaving in August 1974, but in the mode of a special relationship, similar to that of Norway. This means Greek military units would remain under national control during peacetime and revert to NATO direction during wartime. Greece would conditionally participate in military exercises of NATO within and outside the country, as authorised, however, in each case by the Greek government. It should also be possible for other NATO forces to use Greek land, sea and airspace, according to the common needs of the alliance, following authorisation by the Greek government. Nuclear weapons should further remain stored in Greece and nuclear planning should continue for the purpose of supporting operations for the defence of the Greek space.

Greece should continue to participate in the exchange of information between the NATO allies and in the preparation of basic intelligence documents. Apparently Athens realised that its gambit to withdraw from NATO had failed to force the Americans to press Turkey strongly on Cyprus. There also was a strong concern that Turkey could easily promote its claims in the Aegean Sea without Greece in the alliance. This, however, presupposed Turkey's approval and this was not an easy goal to attain. Ankara's initial stance on Greece's application for reintegration into the military wing of NATO was negative but cautious. By pulling out from the exercise WINTEX 75 on the grounds that Greece had denied activity in the Aegean Sea and air space and requesting a reappraisal of NATO infrastructure projects in Greece, Turkey clearly showed that it wanted to impose its own terms. For example, it was opposing the restoration of Greece's pre-1974 operational responsibilities in the Aegean and Athens' access to sensitive intelligence should Greece be relinked to the alliance. By demanding a revision of the US arms embargo towards Turkey, Ankara signalled that its consent was linked to some concessions from the US as well.[12]

Greece's Defence Minister, Evangelos Averof, seems to have worked on Greece's return to NATO since the autumn of 1974. He had assured the Americans that he was planting the seeds for a possible renewed and closer relationship with NATO in the future if circumstances warranted.[13]

US and NATO pressure on Athens appeared to effectuate this partial Greece's U-turn as well. In October 1975, the United States lodged a demarche to the Greek permanent representative to NATO, Theodoropoulos, asking Greece, in a very strong tone and with a hint of blackmail, to clarify its position in NATO by stating simultaneously that the US appreciates Turkey's concerns on major questions posed by ambiguous Greek role in NATO.[14] This followed up on General Secretary of NATO Luns' conversation with Theodoropoulos, in which Luns stressed that Athens should not place NATO in a position of taking the initiative to negotiate a limited role for Greece in the alliance. Athens should make clear what it wanted its relationship with NATO to be, and that negotiations should begin with the question of the unilateral actions Greece had already taken to limit cooperation with NATO.[15]

After some months, there were already the first signs that NATO started positively regarding Greece's request for reintegration into the alliance trying, however, to compensate Turkey for the shortages in its army caused by the US arms embargo. Washington was convinced that this move would enhance the cohesion and credibility of the

alliance at a time when the Soviet power in the area increased, particularly at sea. It was feared that the US arms embargo against Turkey
would inevitably limit the effectiveness of the Turkish armed forces. In
March 1976, the North-Atlantic Assembly recommended the North-
Atlantic Council a) to ensure that the framework of the alliance continues to be available to both parties for settling their disputes; b) to
urge member countries to provide economic assistance to both Greece
and Turkey; c) to examine specifically what measures can be taken by
European members of the alliance to assist Turkey to obtain the spare
parts and equipment it was denied under the embargo.[16]

Turkey also tried to use the negotiations as a means of achieving its
objective to extend its operational control to the West, namely into
areas of responsibility which were under Greek responsibility until
1974, invoking the NATO principle that countries are ultimately
responsible for the defence and the security of their own territories
and peoples. Therefore, the Turks vetoed the initial plans for reintegration, based on pre-1974 arrangements, acceptable to all other allies
and insisted that command boundaries satisfactory to them be agreed
upon before reintegration.[17]

In February 1977, the Turkish representative to NATO informed
the NATO council that Turkey objected to Greek demands and especially Athens' request for a guarantee by other members of the alliance
against the feared danger of Turkish aggression. At the same time,
Ankara stepped up its pressure on the United States to lift its arms
embargo as some sort of compensation for reintegrating Greece into
NATO. Turkey was very much interested in the restructuring of the
LANDSOUTHEAST NATO command at Izmir in a manner that
would allow it to replace the American commander with a Turkish
one and only one American deputy responsible for nuclear matters.[18]

After the initial deliberations, official talks between Greece and
NATO began in March 1978 on 12 issues Athens posed as pre-
requisites for a return and evolved in general around the allocation of
the largest part of the Greek forces to NATO, the maintenance of the
status quo of 1974 regarding the boundaries of operational control,
NATO's defence planning and crisis management and the structure of
NATO commands in the Mediterranean.[19]

Gradually, Greece began disengaging from the special status concept and paving the way for a complete reintegration of Greece into
the military wing of NATO. To that respect, Athens agreed to put at
NATO's disposal the same forces as in the pre-1974 period, especially
the very pivotal for the alliance's anti-aircraft defence systems. What
Athens refused to accept was the inclusion of Greek forces into

defence units, such as those stationed in Turkey, which were under Turkish command. Points of friction also were the new task force concept of the NATO naval forces in the eastern Mediterranean and the use of the Aegean airspace.[20]

Following several months of intensive lobbying by officials of the White House, Department of State and Department of Defence who favoured the lift of the arms embargo on Turkey, in September 1978, a compromise between the US administration and the US legislative power was finally reached. Congress would lift the embargo, provided that the military balance between Greece and Turkey would be fixed at a 7:10 ratio – i.e. Greece would receive 70% of whatever amount was approved for Turkey so that the present at the time balance of military strength was preserved (Katsoulas, 2022, p. 173).

Simultaneously, the US increased the military assistance to Greece in Turkey. In the case of Greece, this military aid was more that it could absorb immediately, enabling Athens to accumulate a large reserve of unused foreign military sales over the years and to fund other major items such as the acquisition of 40 F-16 fighter aircraft from the United States and four frigates from West Germany.[21]

In return, Ankara allowed the United States to resume operations in the military installations where activities had been suspended since the summer of 1975. After productive negotiations, Turkey and the United States fostered their ties in the next years and in March 1980 came to an agreement on defence and economic cooperation (Karaosmanoglu, 1988, p. 299).

The negotiations on Greece's return to NATO, however, did not make any significant progress. Following a series of exploratory talks between Generals Davou and Haig between March and May 1978, a preliminary agreement on the disposition of Greek Forces to the North-Atlantic alliance had been struck, which had been approved by all alliance countries except Turkey and therefore did not materialise. In February 1979, US President Carter tried to boost the negotiations by sending an official letter to Karamanlis informing him about the US support for the consultations among military leaders aimed at removing the obstacles that had prevented the completion of Greece's reintegration into NATO.[22]

Consequently, the SACEUR submitted to the Greek government three successive proposals aimed at regulating Greece's reintegration to NATO which tried to accommodate the wishes of Greece and Turkey on the question of command and control arrangements in the Aegean: the first, submitted in March 1979, required Greece: a) to make a disclaimer that any arrangements within NATO would not be considered as a precedent in the bilateral disputes between Greece and Turkey; b) to recognise 6 nautical miles of airspace and not 10 while using the airspace for military purposes, c) to accept full exchange of information by all available means, automatically and manually between the Larissa and Izmir headquarters and d) to open the Aegean airways to Turkey, if Turkey would do that same (this component was accepted by Greece by not by Turkey). Greece rejected the proposal and thus the SACEUR came up with a new one in May 1979, which, in essence, overturned the Davou–Haig agreement. The new one required Greece to accept the creation of two zones for air defence, one over continental national territory and another only for the Aegean Sea as well as the creation in Larissa of an advanced echelon controlled by the NATO command in Izmir. This proposal was immediately rejected by Greece as well. Then the SACEUR came up with a third proposal in which the air defence coordination responsibilities of the NATO command in Izmir were limited, whereas Greek and Turkish authorities would be responsible for any activity within their territorial waters. Nevertheless, the new proposal was considered to be detrimental to the defence of Greece and even worse than what was in force before 1974 as there were no clear command boundaries leading for sure to friction. Athens was afraid that it would be compelled to accept Turkish co-responsibility in the Aegean. Given the 2,316 Greek islands, islets and rocky islets, each of which has its own coastal zone, creating corresponding zones of national waters, this arrangement, so feared by Athens, would inhibit Greece from extending its territorial waters from 6 to 12 nautical miles.[23]

In February 1980, the SACEUR submitted his "Proposal for the Immediate Return of Greece to the Alliance's Integrated Military Structure".[24] Greece continued to insist that the pre-1974 boundaries be the basis for assigning missions and areas of responsibilities to appropriate NATO headquarters. Turkey insisted that the pre-1974 boundaries were unsatisfactory and had been illegally drawn. This, in conjunction with Greek withdrawal, so Ankara asserted, had rendered those boundaries null and void. The novel element in this proposal was to set the boundary issue aside for resolution in the future. It suggested, among others, that air defence procedures would be in accordance with the SHAPE directive on NATO European Integrated Air Defence: hot pursuit of a hostile, or an unidentified aircraft, into the territorial airspace of either Greece or Turkey would not be allowed under any circumstances without the expressed permission of the nation concerned. Air identifications or intercepts would be conducted either:

1 By Greek aircraft under Greek ground control.
2 By Turkish aircraft under Turkish ground control.
3 By Greek aircraft under Turkish ground control.
4 By Turkish aircraft under Greek ground control.

In accordance with ICAO rules, the military aircraft of both countries would be required to report when entering a Flight Information Region and conduct itself with due regard to air safety. Operational orders for exercises would specifically list all preplanned flights, including times on station, and clearly delineate the NOTAM areas where they would be flown. Greece would cancel NOTAM 1157 simultaneously with the Turkish cancellation of NOTAM 714.[25]

Ahead of the General Election of 1981 in Greece and given the great lead in the polls for the anti-NATO disposed socialist party, the incumbent conservative government started pushing for a quick conclusion of the negotiations. Thus, it warned that the application to rejoin would be necessarily withdrawn if there was no agreement by the turn of 1980 to 1981 as well as the NATO-connected US military bases in Greece would have to close. Athens also made a strong plea to the British Prime Minister to pressure Turkey to lift the veto on Greek reintegration. In early October 1980, the US diplomats informed the Greek Foreign Minister Konstantinos Mitsotakis that they realised that the forthcoming Greek elections made an early resolution of the issue even more desirable, but the United States were not prepared to exercise pressure on Turkey to that end. The issue would have to be resolved by the Greeks and Turks themselves. The future of the US bases in Greece was a matter for the Greek government. London and Washington believed that Greece behaved inconsistently undermining the negotiations, as the Greeks could not accept anything but a simple return to pre-1974 command arrangements. In private conversations with Greek politicians and diplomats, the British and Americans did not fail to mention that President Carter himself was very upset by the Greek "foot-dragging". The British Prime Minister Margaret Thatcher also pressed at the same time the Greek Prime Minister Rallis to support SACEUR's efforts to negotiate a solution and to hold out against the domestic opposition.[26]

In September 1980, the Turkish armed forces carried out a coup d'état, headed by Chief of the General Staff General Kenan Evren, allegedly to end the political violence between far-left, far-right (Grey Wolves), Islamist militant groups, and the state. Unexpectedly, the new military regime in Turkey proved very conciliatory towards NATO and Athens and willing to let Greece take a back seat in the Defence

Planning Committee, thereby leaving all outstanding issues to be discussed later.[27] Having many open fronts at home and abroad and under pressure to consolidate their position in power, the Turkish generals most probably deemed it necessary to settle an issue that burdened Turkey's relationship with its NATO allies.

Reintegration of Greece was indeed made possible in October 1980, after long and arduous negotiations, on the basis of the aforementioned SACEUR "Proposal", known as the *Rogers Plan* within a context of "constructive ambiguity" and a mutually tolerable compromise for Greece and Turkey. The *Rogers Plan* legal formula was not to call for any specific areas of naval command, but rather allow the overall NATO sea commander to call upon either nation's forces as needed. The establishment of two new Allied Commands with headquarters in Larissa was also provided: the Land Forces South-Central Europe (LANDSOUTHCENT) and Seventh Allied Tactical Air Force (7ATAF) for land and air operations forces respectively, with Greek commanders, across the Allied Land Forces South-Eastern Europe (LANDSOUTHEAST) in Izmir, which was under Turkish command since 1978. The commander of the Greek air military force and the naval military force would be in charge of the same area of operational responsibility as before 1974. The new status of Greece and Turkey within the alliance was completely independent from the Greek-Turkish bilateral relations. Regarding the contribution of Greek military forces to NATO, Athens offered more air military forces than it was required in order to demonstrate its upgraded capabilities and to secure more money from the alliance for infrastructure projects related to the Greek air force.[28]

The international context proved very conducive. The fall of the Shah of Iran in February 1979, the Soviet nuclear and conventional forces' build-up in Europe, the Soviet invasion of Afghanistan in December 1979 and the death of Tito in May 1980 seem to have facilitated this development (Rizas, 2008, p. 64).

As the *Washington Post* wrote at that time, politically, the reintegration of the Greek forces was viewed as an extremely timely boost to NATO's frequently battered solidarity and could not have come at a better time with the turmoil continuing in nearby Southwest Asia, shoring up NATO's vital southern flank. It also was a valuable success for the Carter administration at a crucial time (Washington Post, 1980).

In his report to the NATO ministerial meeting of December 1980, the Secretary General of NATO, Joseph Luns, expressed his satisfaction with the improvement in the climate of relations between Greece and Turkey which, in particular, had made possible the return of Greece to NATO's integrated military structure. This development remedied, according to Luns, a disturbing weakness on the south-eastern Flank of the alliance and restored the fabric of Atlantic solidarity in a region so important from every aspect to the security of the alliance.[29]

Luns' optimism was premature. The provisions of the *Rogers Plan* turned out to be a source of continuous friction. In the following years, both Greece and Turkey, interpreted the provisions completely differently. They constantly disagreed on the respective responsibility boundaries of the Larisa and Izmir commands. Turkey believed that the new boundaries of the operational responsibility in the Aegean were temporary, while Greece considered them as an inviolable condition of Greece's reintegration (Veremis, 2000, pp. 345–349).

Although Greece started participating again in the military drills of the alliance, Ankara never accepted the boundaries of operational responsibility of the 28th Tactical Airforce as boundaries of the 7ATAF, as they were different from the boundaries of operational responsibility of the command of the land forces of south-eastern Europe which was located in Izmir. NATO tried to establish first the headquarters of the 7ATAF and then to define the boundaries in order to avoid Ankara's reactions. This issue, however, remained a source of problems.[30]

Notes

1 US Department of State released documents in 2005: "Telegram from the US Embassy to NATO to the Secretary of State in Washington 15 August 1974, Subject: Greece, NATO, and the US – Some Reflections".
2 Averof Archive: folder 30: "Brief Memorandum of Averof on his Meeting with Giulio Andreotti, 10 September 1974". It is noteworthy that Averof warned Andreotti that a possible delivery of warplanes that were being constructed in Italy could impair the Greek–Italian relations.
3 Averof Archive: folder 38a: "Report of the General Staff of Armed Forces on the Political and Military Structure of NATO 7 August 1975".
4 Karamanlis Archive: Folder 9, Greek-Turkish Relations: "Brief Memorandum by the Greek Minister of Defence for the Head of the Government 6 January 1975 on Greece's Withdrawal from NATO".
5 US Department of State releases 2005: "Message from the Secretary of State in Washington to the US mission to NATO, Subject: Greece and NATO; Greek Withdrawal and Reply to Karamanlis Letter, September 1974".
6 Averof Archive: Folder 38a: "Minutes of the 22and Session in 1975 of the Supreme Council of the Hellenic Armed Forces. Subject: Greece's relation with NATO".

7   US Department of State releases 2005: "Telegram from Secretary of State in Washington DC to the US Mission to NATO and all NATO Countries Capitals, Subject: Greece-NATO Infrastructure, 28 September 1974".

8   Wikileaks: https://wikileaks.org/plusd/cables/1978ATHENS01377_d.html. "US Department of State. Defense Minister Discusses Nuclear Weapons in Greece Control of US bases, and charges of American Military Interference in Cyprus Crisis During Parliamentary Interpellation, 15 February 1978".

9   Karamanlis Archive: Folder 2b: "Report Without Date on the Negotiations Of Withdrawal"; US Department of State releases 2005: "Telegram from the US mission to NATO to the Secretary of State and to all US embassies in NATO countries 19 September 1974, Subject: Greece and NATO"; US Department of State releases 2006: "Telegram from the FM US Mission to NATO to the Secretary of State in Washington, 18 September 1974".

10 Averof Archive: Folder 55: "Joint Declaration of Intent between Evangelos Averof, Minister of the National Defence of the Hellenic State and Carl Kotchian, President of Lockheed Aircraft Corporation of Los Angeles"; (Stergiou, 2021, p. 116).

11 NATO Archive: Document DRC-DS (76)9 PD: "NATO Defence Review Committee, Meeting Held at NATO Headquarters in Brussels, on 9 April 1976".

12 Already in October 1974, the Greek Foreign Ministry had warned that this strategy was very risky, jeopardised Greece's defence capabilities and undermined the country's efforts to attain the status of the full member of the European Community and, in general, Greece's position in the Western world. Karamanlis Archive: Folder 5: "Note of the Greek Foreign Ministry, 16 October 1974"; Folder 35b: "Report of the Greek Permanent Representative to NATO, Vyron Theodoropoulos, on his Speech at the NATO Council, 9 October 1975"; (Rizas, 2008, pp. 60–61).

13 US Department of State, 2005 releases: "Telegram from the Secretary of State in Washington to the US Embassy in London 29 October 1974".

14 US Department of State releases 2006: "Telegram from the Secretary of State in Washington to the US Embassies in Athens and Ankara, Subject: Greece and NATO and US Security Assistance to Greece, 14 October 1975".

15 US Department of State releases 2006: "Telegram from the US Mission to NATO to the Secretary of State in Washington, Subject: Greece-NATO relations, 6 October 1975".

16 NATO Archive: Document PO 76/15: "Secretary General's Report to the Permanent Representatives on Recommendations and Resolutions Adopted at the 21the Session of the North Atlantic Assembly 12 March 1976".

17 Karamanlis Archive: Folder 35⊠: "Diplomatic Office of the Prime Minister, Notice on NATO and Greece 1982 (Top Secret)".

18 State Department 2005 releases: "Telegram of the US Mission to NATO to the Secretary of State in Washington, Subject: Greek Reply to NATO on Greece-NATO Relations: Turkish Reaction, 15 February 1997".

19 Karamanlis Archive: Folder 35⊠: "Notice on the Re-Integration of Greece into the Integrated NATO structure 1982".

20 Karamanlis Archive: Folder 5b: "Translation of the NATO Military Committee's Assessment over the Future Relations Ship between Greece

and the Integrated Military Structure of the Alliance after the Meetings between the SACEUR and Greek militaries, July 1978".

21 CIA releases 2017: "Memorandum on the Military Balance between Greece and Turkey; How It Stands, Where It Is Headed, What It Means, June 1988".

22 Karamanlis Archive: Folder 59: "US President Carter's Letter to Karamanlis, 28 February 1979".

23 Karamanlis Archive: Folder 43: "NATO (June 1979)"; Folder 20B NATO-Greece (1974–1978), "Negotiations on Greece's Withdrawal".

24 Karamanlis Archive: Folder 42: "SACEUR's Proposal for the Immediate Return of Greece to the Alliance's Integrated Military Structure, 11 February 1980".

25 Both NOTAMs had been issued during the Cyprus Crisis in the Summer 1974 and had essentially burdened the aviation over eastern Mediterranean.

26 PRO: FCO 9/2965, Greece and NATO: "Correspondence between Foreign and Commonwealth Office, the British Permanent Representation to NATO and British Embassies in Athens, Washington and Ankara during September and October 1980".

27 Ibidem.

28 Karamanlis Archive: Folder 35⊠: "General Staff of the Hellenic Army, Study on the Relations between Greece and NATO December 1981 (Top Secret)".

29 NATO Archive: "Document P0/80/110: Secretary General's Report on his Watching Brief (on the Greek-Turkish Relations) to the December 1980 Ministerial Meeting, 1 December 1980".

30 Karamanlis Archive: Folder 35⊠: "Notice on the Re-Integration of Greece into the Integrated NATO Structure, 1982".

References

Primary Sources

Karamanlis Archive
NATO Archive
Foreign Office Archive
CIA Releases 2017
US Department of State Releases

Secondary Sources

Congressional Research Service Library of Congress, 1975. Greece and Turkey: Some military implications related to NATO and the Middle East. Report prepared for the special Subcommittee on Investigations of the Committee on Foreign Affairs. Washington: US Government Printing Office.

Karaosmanoglu, A., 1988. Turkey and the southern flank: Domestic and external contexts. In J. Chipman (ed.), *NATO's Southern allies: Internal and*

External Challenges. An Atlantic Institute for International Affairs Research Volume (pp. 287–353). London and New York: Routledge.

Katsoulas, S., 2022. *The United States and Greek-Turkish Relations. The Guardian's Dilemma*. London and New York: Routledge.

Klapsis, A., 2011. From Dictatorship to Democracy: US-Greek Relations at a Critical Turning Point (1974–1975). *Mediterranean Quarterly*, 22 (1), 61–73.

Kollias, Ch., 1995. The effects of external security considerations on defence expenditure in the context of Greek-Turkish bilateral relations. *Bogazici Journal Review of Social, Economic and Administrative Studies*, 9 (1), 135–147.

Kontos, M., 2016. Foreign Interventions and Greek Cypriot Perceptions. In Warner, J., Lovell, D. and Kontos M., *Contemporary Social and Political Aspects of the Cyprus Problem* (pp. 36–56). Newcastle upon Tyne: Cambridge Scholars Publishing.

Papadimitriou, D., 2007. George Papadopoulos and the Dictatorship of the Colonels, 1967–1974. In B. Fischer (ed.), *Balkan Strongmen. Dictators and Authoritarian Rulers of South-Eastern Europe (pp. 393–424)*. West Lafayette, Indiana: Purdue University Press.

Rizas, S., 2008. Atlanticism and Europeanism in Greek foreign and security policy in the 1970s. *Southeast European and Black Sea Studies*, 8 (1), 51–66.

Stergiou, A., 2021. *Greece's Ostpolitik. Dealing With the "Devil"*. Contribution to the International Relations. Switzerland AG: Springer Nature.

Veremis, T., 2000. Oi Ellinotourkikes Sheseis 1974–1981 [Greek–Turkish relations 1974–1981]. In G. Christopoulos & I. Bastias (eds.), *Istoria tou Ellinikou Ethnous* [*History of the Greek Nation*], vol. 16 (pp. 345–349). Athens: Ekdodiki Publisher.

Washington Post, 1980. Return of Greece to NATO military alliance hailed by US, 21 October.

4 The evolution of the Cyprus question in the 1970s and 1980s

Cementing the division

The division had devastating effects on the whole island. The Greek Cypriots living in the north were forced to move south and the Turkish Cypriots living in the south were forced to move to the north. Practically, one-third of the island's population became refugees in their own country. The forceful creation of two separate ethnic zones demarcated by the heavily fortified so-called *Attila Line* eliminated any interaction between the two sides for the decades that followed (Joseph, 2005, p. 49).

The Gross Domestic Product of the Cyprus Republic dropped by 70%. Important farming areas such as Morphou, the home of the island's citrus industry, and most of the once famous tourism accommodation came under Turkish-Cypriot control. The port of Famagusta remained out of service and the main international airport in Nicosia was turned into an UN-controlled buffer zone. Nevertheless, the southern part, contrary to the occupied part, prospered in the next years economically due to a rapid development of trade, tourism, and shipping, but also due to its transformation into a robust and reliable offshore centre (Stergiou, 2023).

With the onset of prosperity, the *Enosis* ideology faded away, as ideological dependency on the "Greek national center" declined. Anger, resentments and feelings of betrayal filled many Greek Cypriots about Athens' attitude during the Turkish invasion. The protection of the integrity and the independence of the Republic began gaining ground at the expense of the use of Hellenic national symbols and the once dominant demand for union with Greece as the ultimate goal of Cypriot self-determination (Loizides, 2007, p. 177).

In the north, the *de facto* division of the island favoured the rise of Turkish nationalism that turned out to be the grand narrative of legitimising the partition. In this search for legitimacy, a new national discourse was adopted reducing the Turkish-Cypriot community to

DOI: 10.4324/9781003350033-5

"just the Turks who happened to live in Cyprus". In this official ideological narrative, the existence of the Turkish Cypriots as a different community was not only denied but also regarded as treason against the Turkish nation. Only a few sporadic contacts between mainlanders run counter to this official discourse of sameness and organic unity of the Turkish nation (Kizilyürek, 2005, p. 239).

The levels and types of attachment to Turkey changed significantly in the 1980s due to international isolation, Turkey's interference in Turkish-Cypriot community affairs, economic stagnation, and the colonisation of Cyprus by Turkish settlers (Loizides, 2007, p. 177). While Greek Cypriots continued developing a more independent identity, differentiating themselves from mainland Greeks, in the northern part of Cyprus, the "Cypriotness" of Turkish Cypriots began to face the challenge of their new "internal" others. This notion was coined to describe the Turkish settlers, the illegal immigrant workers, and the Turkish army that were stationed or settled down in the north after 1974 (Féron and Lisaniler, 2009, p. 207).

As a matter of fact, through the settlement of Turks or Turkophones, and sometimes other ethnicities from Bulgaria, Anatolia and the Black Sea by the Turkish state the northern part underwent, in violation of international law, a total demographic and therefore social and cultural transformation. In this way, Ankara attempted to enhance its control in the northern part and to change the constituency in favour of its proxy politicians. Moreover, a massive process of Turkification entailing the changing of 3,000 old *toponymies*, the building of mosques and the conversion of churches into mosques took place. Turkish forces consolidated their position on the island and a military airfield was developed. Both developments regarding the Turkish break-away regime in 1976 and in 1983, the European Court of Human Rights found Turkey guilty of repeated violations of the European Convention on Human Rights in regard to the "TRNC" (Stergiou, 2012, pp. 57–79).

This move was not only about to ensure that the TRNC complied with Turkish government policies, Turkey attempted to manage the balance of power in the occupied part of Cyprus by settling non-Cypriots. It also achieved a few other goals. For instance, numerous individuals with criminal records were disposed of there. Aside from seasonal labourers, the majority of the early settlers to northern Cyprus in the 1970s were those looking to leave their past behind (criminals, prostitutes, etc.). They were immediately naturalised as citizens of the TRNC and became eligible to vote.[1]

On the other hand, the Greek side succeeded in gaining the United Nations', European Economic Community's, Council of Europe's and the Non-Aligned Movement's support against Turkey's second offensive and the prolonged stay of Turkish troops on the island. In response, the Turkish side has been refusing to-date to recognise the Republic of Cyprus, diminishing it to merely an administration representing the Greek community, in the same way as the Turkish-Cypriot administration represents the Turkish-Cypriot chunk of the overall Cypriot population.

Initially, while Ankara presented itself as very upset about the "unfair" diplomatic isolation, signalled, unofficially, in the fall of 1974, it did show readiness to make some gestures of goodwill and to allow, under certain conditions, a limited return of Greek-Cypriot refugees to the occupied areas and the establishment of a federal state.[2]

In 1975, however, to the dismay of the Greek Cypriots, the Turkish Cypriots established the Turkish federated State of Cyprus, indicating their wish to participate again in a single state entity with the Greek Cypriots only as an equal part in a loose Cypriot federation, whereas Ankara began infusing essential financial aid to the north to develop its separate infrastructure and economy (Bahcheli, 1989, pp. 110–113).

Furthermore, Athens tried to elicit support from various countries for its cause in Cyprus, beginning with the neighbouring states. At first, Greece approached the regional Arab Islamic countries, since the Greek State for various political and economic reasons had followed an Arab-friendly and a *de facto* not friendly to Israel policy since the end of World War II (Stergiou, 2015, p. 418). In September 1974, Averof complained to the Vice-President of the Egyptian government, Abdel Aziz Mohamed Hegazy, about Egypt's neutrality on the Cyprus issue and material assistance to Turkey, while Greece was faced with reprisals by Israel and powerful Zionists because of its Arab-friendly policy. The Egyptians could, however, not sever their ties with Turkey, but presented themselves ready to support the demand for demilitarisation of the island, if this included the British Sovereign Bases as well.[3]

In the meeting of the NATO Council of Ministers (a body of the political structure of NATO in which Greece still took part) in Brussels in December 1974, Dimitris Bitsios, the Greek Minister for Foreign Affairs, informed his colleagues that the Greek-Cypriot side was ready to negotiate with the Turkish-Cypriot side to be represented by Rauf Denktash on a possible solution of the Cyprus tragedy that had affected tens of thousands of people. He hoped that the other side would show a little goodwill and a spirit of cooperation. M. Esenbel, the Turkish Minister of Foreign Affairs, retorted that it was a fact that ... *the Turkish Cypriots who had been living in Cyprus, according to the clauses of international treaties and under a Constitution elaborated by the two sides, had been deprived of the right to which they were entitled under that Constitution and, in 1963, 1967 and again in 1974, had been faced with the threat of subjugation ... Turkey had been most reluctant to resort to the measures which she had taken in 1974, but that she had felt duty-bound to fulfil her obligations under the international treaties that had created the independent State of Cyprus. A new situation had now arisen where the objective was to obtain a settlement through peaceable means which would be just and would satisfy the needs of all the interested parties ...* Canada that was the second largest contributor to the peacekeeping force stationed on the island since 1964 assured NATO members that his country informed the council an it wished to continue its support as long as it seemed productive to do so, although that support was becoming increasingly difficult to sustain.[4]

Indeed, in 1975, the two communities began carrying out talks aimed at finding a comprehensive solution to the Cyprus Problem and supposedly reunifying the island. After repeated rounds of discussions between Makarios and the Turkish-Cypriot leader, Rauf Denktaş, a major break-through was achieved in January 1977, when the two sides reached an agreement (the High-Level Agreement) designed to remodel Cyprus into a bi-zonal and bi-communal federal state. However, the Turkish-Cypriot insistence on bi-zonality "as the basis of political equality as well as the security of their people" reflected the geographical division of the island (Balkir & Yalma, 2009, p. 51) and hence was a step towards the consolidation of the political division.

The term "bi-zonal" identified two areas with a Greek-Cypriot and a Turkish-Cypriot administration, respectively. The term "bi-communal" indicated that the two communities would participate effectively in the organs and decisions of the central federal government, while the specific meaning of the word "effectively" had yet to be defined. The new state would have one single sovereignty, one single citizenship and one single international personality. For a transitional period, freedom of movement and settlement would be restricted.[5]

Four months later, however, in August 1977, Makarios died and negotiations restarted. He was replaced by Spyros Kyprianou, the former Foreign Minister, who was President of the House of Representatives at the time of Makarios' death. Kyprianou took over the negotiations for the Greek-Cypriot side. In 1979 the two sides reached a new agreement, which re-affirmed the 1977 High-Level Agreement, but also included provisions for the demilitarisation of the island and a commitment to refrain from destabilising actions. Nevertheless, shortly after, Denktash demanded that the Turkish-Cypriot federal state be exclusively Turkish-Cypriot and the Greek-Cypriot state be exclusively Greek Cypriot, indicating rather the revival of the "two-state solution", which torpedoed the agreement, although these two agreements, which were accepted by the international community, theoretically remained the basis of future talks (Papapolyviou, 2021, pp. 12–13).

Developments in the Middle East during 1982 underlined once again the strategic importance of Cyprus and the security situation in this area as a vital component for the cohesion and harmony between the two NATO allies on the south-eastern flank. In the 1980s, some American politicians believed that the Cyprus Problem could not be isolated from other issues between Greece and Turkey. Thus, it should be put into "one basket" and dealt with other disputes in the Aegean, such as the air space and continental shelf (package deal).[6]

Greece's new Prime Minister Andreas Papandreou appeared to share this view and tried to raise the Cyprus issue emphatically in the international fora. For example, during the Poland crisis in 1982, he criticised the Western countries "for their reaction to the situation in Poland, although they had shown no reaction at all against the impo-sition of Martial Law in Cyprus and the continuing invasion by Turkish troops of Cyprus".[7]

On the other hand, Turkey became more and more assertive towards Cyprus. In 1982–1983, Ankara threatened to launch a new military operation against the Cyprus Republic under the pretext that the latter provided shelter to members of the Armenian liberation organisations fleeing from Beirut after the Israeli invasion of South Lebanon in the summer of 1982. Though investigations carried out by the UN peacekeeping force stationed in Cyprus did not confirm these allegations, Ankara continued threatening. The situation was further aggravated by the simultaneous failure of the then-UN mediation efforts aimed at finding a solution to the Cyprus Problem. Moreover, in November 1983, the Turkish-Cypriot leadership took advantage of the post-election political instability in Turkey and unilaterally declared the independence to the break-away regime. The military had been three years in power in Turkey and were about to hand over to a civilian government. Turkish-Cypriot hardliner Leader Denktash saw in the very brief period of interregnum an opportunity to attain what he had been fighting for in his whole life, the establishment of a sepa-rate Turkish-Cypriot state in Cyprus, although this ran counter to the agreements he had signed with Makarios and Kyprianou in 1977 and

1979. Although the so-called Turkish Republic of Northern Cyprus (TRNC) as the new state called itself, was soon recognised by Turkey, the rest of the international community condemned the move. Within days, the UN Security Council passed a resolution (by a 14–1 vote; only Pakistan opposed) declaring the act "legally invalid" and calling for the withdrawal of the unilateral declaration of independence, calling at the same time on all states not to recognise any Cypriot state other than the Republic of Cyprus. As a further step to consolidate the Turkish-Cypriot state the parliamentary assembly of the TRNC adopted a new Constitution on 12 March 1985, which after publication and public comment, was put to a referendum on 5 May. It was approved by 70%. In the new Constitution, there was no reference in it to the establishment of a federal Republic of Cyprus (Dodd, 2010, pp. 147–157).

The establishment of the TRNC constituted a major affront to Greece. Greek strategy planners feared that a possible recognition of the break-away regime by other soverign states could aggravate the Turkish threat in the Aegean which also was expected to become more immediate and menacing. Once again, the Cyprus Problem posed a highly inflammatory issue for the US foreign policy and the NATO allies. Even before the declaration of independence (in June 1983), CIA analysts noted that the possibility of a war between Greece and Turkey should be taken seriously. Their disputes would spill over into other areas, hindering agreement between Athens and Ankara on NATO commands and control responsibilities in the Aegean, heightening bilateral tensions over Cyprus and other issues. The most likely spark for conflict would be an accident, probably an inadvertent air clash, which could lead to extended air-to-air combat or even escalate into combined air, naval and ground operations in the Aegean. Superior equipment and training would give the Greeks an edge in air and naval combat in the Aegean, while superior numbers would give the Turks a clear-cut advantage in Cyprus.[8]

In February 1984, Papandreou publicly claimed that Athens and Nicosia had won a worldwide diplomatic victory following Denktash's declaration of independence that only Turkey had recognised. Moreover, Athens informed its allies that both Greeks and Greek Cypriots were concerned by the lack of progress on the Cyprus Problem "due to the very negative stance the Turkish had been adopting". It also called them "to fulfil their responsibilities and in particular to put pressure on Turks". As the allies did not accommodate Greek wishes, a few months later, Papandreou overtly criticised them and the international community for not supporting Kyprianou's set of ideas although this contained concessions towards Turkey and instead exerting. pressure on Nicosia and not on Ankara to give in.[9]

In response to the proclamation of the TRNC, the Greek authorities made public their intention not to allow anybody with a TRNC passport or of persons holding a passport showing evidence of a visit to enter Greece.[10] The exchange of Ambassadors between the TRNC and Turkey in April 1984 also was met with a fierce reaction from Athens threatening that this act might have very serious repercussions and appealed to Greece's allies to take measures against Turkey, warning that Greece would wait to see the form that the allies' action would take.[11]

In March 1984, the Secretary General of the United Nations Pérez de Guéllar who had been the United National Special Representative on the island in the years 1976–1977, called for "proximity talks" between the two communities within the framework of the federal solution agreed in 1977 and 1979. Guéllar also submitted to the Leader of the Turkish-Cypriot Community Rauf Denktash and the Foreign Minister of the Republic of Cyprus Giorgos Iakovou a "five-point plan" with the aim of unlocking the stalemate. The draft agreement did not resolve all outstanding issues but practically paved the way for new settlements in the future heralding a break-through, if not a solution. Among others, the proclamation of the so-called Turkish Republic of Northern Cyprus should be frozen. Neither of the sides should enhance its military presence on the island and the Varosha area (the abandoned ghost tourist resort city on the south coast of Cyprus which was, however, *de facto* under the Turkish army's control) should be put under UN control with the option to deliver it at a later stage to the owners of the houses and the hotels. At the time, the talks were labelled very promising by the international community. This expectation proved to be fallacious. The Turkish Cypriots demanded a rotating presidency, which the Turkish Cypriots considered a prerequisite of political equality and the territorial question turned out to be an insurmountable obstacle. The Turkish Cypriots were reluctant to lower their share below 32%, whereas the Greek Cypriots were not willing to surrender more than the share of the Turkish Cypriots in the overall population in the 1960s, which means 18% (Bahcheli, 1989, pp. 118–121; Tzermias, 1998, p. 573).

In order to facilitate the agreement, Washington linked the approval of the US Senate for military aid to Turkey to the handover of Varosha to the United Nations Peacekeeping Force in Cyprus. The Greek-Cypriot side accepted the plan but Denktash[12] procrastinated characteristically in his response, while the Turkish military in Ankara did not even deign to discuss the American proposition.[13]

Moreover, the Senate Foreign Relations Committee attachment of Cyprus-related conditions to US aid for Turkey prompted universal condemnation in Turkey, enforcing the anti-American resentment. As the British embassy in Ankara reported, the Turks were furious about the respective American move labelling it as "bribery, blackmail and pressure". They believed that it was both dangerous and mistaken to use aid, which served a mutual objective as a pressure point in matters that have nothing to do with it. This would solely make the Cyprus Problem more difficult to solve by obliging the Turks *to re-evaluate the situation ... in order not to appear as if they are granting a concession under pressure ... and by pushing the Greek Cypriots into dreaming and imagining things that can never happen ...* Nevertheless, Turkish Prime Minister Özal announced some goodwill gestures towards Greece. However, as the British Ambassador in Athens noted, this move seemed to be of no practical value whatsoever and therefore he correctly feared that, with some justification, the Greeks would regard this gesture as no more than a tactical move designed to conceal underlying inflexibility.[14]

On 16 March 1984, the UN Secretary General saw Denktash in New York. He had been trying to persuade both sides to accept a three-point proposal this time: an improved offer by the Turkish Cypriots on Varosha; a freeze on the "internationalisation of the Cyprus Problem" by the Greek Cypriots meaning the campaign against the proclaimed Turkish Republic of Northern Cyprus and equally on the implementation of unilateral declaration of independence by the Turkish Cypriots; a resumption of the intercommunal dialogue. Denktash played for time in New York saying that he wanted to consult Ankara and the Turkish-Cypriot community, while criticising the Senate Foreign Relations Committee recommendation on military aid to Turkey. Following Turkish press reports of Greek contingency plans to reinforce southern Cyprus with a Greek army division, the Turkish government also stated that it had no intention of tolerating any upset in the military balance in Cyprus.[15]

According to the Turks, there was a structural problem in Greek–Turkish relations, Papandreou's personal handling of major foreign policy issues and the absence of a normal bureaucratic machine that increased the risk of impetuous action. Papandreou's actions were, according to the Turks, influenced by domestic political preoccupations and the need to revive support for his Socialist party PASOK ahead of the European Parliament elections.[16]

In the next months, Athens and Ankara sharpened their rhetoric, even exchanging threats against each other. The situation escalated to such a degree that some British officials feared a possible accidental confrontation in the buffer zone in Cyprus, which would probably emanate from a Turkish initiative to be immediately responded to by the Greek side. In particular, they feared that the leader of the Turkish-Cypriot community Rauf Denktash could spark an escalation prompting the reaction of the Republic of Cyprus. The British estimated, however, that the Turkish government for all the freedom of action it had given to him, continued to keep careful control over any moves by Denktash which could involve the Turkish armed forces in Cyprus. For the foreseeable future, no improvement in the Greek–Turkish relations, which could lead to an easing of the problems NATO was confronted with, was expected. Even NATO Secretary General Lord Carrington's visit to Ankara in June 1984 failed to smooth the waters.[17]

In the mid-1980s, in its capacity as the main defence organisation of Western Europe, NATO participated in the Stockholm Conference on Confidence- and Security-Building Measures and Disarmament in Europe convened in the context of the Conference on Security and Cooperation in Europe (CSCE). Within this framework, the Western countries tried to push through some mutually complementary confidence- and security-building measures, providing among others for: the exchange of information about the organisation and location of military forces in the area of applicability; exchange of annual forecasts of notifiable military activities, etc.[18]

The conference, however, also provided the terrain for a clash between Turkey and Greece on the issue of the representation of Cyprus at the CSCE. In September 1986, Turkey submitted interpretative statements recorded in Journal No. 379 of the concluding 178th Plenary Meeting according to which at that time in Cyprus existed two separate political entities: in the north, the Turkish Republic of Northern Cyprus that was the exclusive, sole and legitimate authority and represented the Turkish people of Cyprus and in the south, the Greek-Cypriot administration having only the authority to speak on behalf of the Greek Cypriots. Hence, there was not a single authority representing the whole of Cyprus and its peoples. Therefore, Turkey declared that the CSCE Stockholm decisions would have no validity or applicability as regards and in relation to Cyprus, since the representation of Cyprus at the CSCE was neither legal nor legitimate. Against this reservation Nicosia and Athens reiterated previous statements according to which the Turkish invasion of the Republic of Cyprus did not qualify Turkey to dispute the legitimacy of the government of the Republic of Cyprus that was recognised by the community of nations, the United Nations and the other international organisations as the sole and legitimate authority representing the whole of Cyprus. The Turkish Republic of Northern Cyprus was an entity which did not exist according to the UN Security Council Resolutions 541 (1983) and 550 (1984). Eventually, the government of the Republic of Cyprus adopted the Document of the Stockholm Conference on the reservation that "it was binding upon the whole of Cyprus, as it had been given by the representative of the legitimate Government of Cyprus".[19]

In 1986 and 1987, Turkey applied for full membership in the European Community with a view to reviving the association process that had been frozen in response to the 1980 military coup. Athens tried hard to link Turkey's application to the Cyprus Problem. To that purpose, it opposed the fourth Financial EC-Turkey protocol of 600 million ECU's on the grounds that Turkey occupied part of another country associated with the EC and vetoed the resumption of the association process. The Council of the European Community overrode the Greek veto through the use of a majority decision, but Greece pursued the case further by appealing against the Commission in the European Court of Justice. Not accidentally, also in 1987, the Cyprus Republic, which had been associated with the European Community (EC) since 1972, established with the support of Greece a Customs Union regime with the EC with the strong support of Greece that paradoxically was transformed from a Europe-sceptical country to a Europe-friendly country. Athens's primary political objective was to motivate the EC to undertake initiatives aimed at finding a solution to the Cyprus Problem, since Turkey aspired at the same time to become a full member of the European Community (Kranidiotis, 1992, pp. 183–184).

In May 1988, the European Parliament passed a resolution declaring "Turkey's unlawful occupation of Northern Cyprus as a major stumbling block to the normalisation of EC relations with Turkey". The European Parliament's resolution was espoused by the European Commission in 1989, which rejected Turkey's application stating that Turkey was not ready for membership stating a string of factors against Turkey's admission. The Greek–Turkish conflict and the Cyprus Problem were included in these factors (Rumelili, 2008, pp. 94–128).

On 4 May 1988, Özal, in an interview, blamed the collapse of negotiations with the EC on German Foreign Minister Genscher, who had believed that Turkey would accept the Cyprus Problem being put on the agenda. On 20 May, the European Parliament called on the EC

Foreign Ministers to put pressure on Turkey so that Ankara would present a precise timetable for the withdrawal of its troops and settlers. Özal reacted immediately. In an interview with the newspaper Hurriyet on 22 May, he declared his unwillingness to discuss the Cyprus Problem on this basis (Richter, 2021, pp. 70–72).

It was obvious, that the Turks were not willing to yield to any international pressure, no matter how intensive this was, and accept a settlement that entailed forfeiture of the valuable prize they won in 1974.

Notes

1 The Cyprus State Archives, Archive of the Foreign Ministry (Henceforth cited as Cyprus State Archive): Folder FA 2/311-312-313: "Turkish Cypriot Opposition in the 1980s".

2 Averof Archive: Folder 34: "Memorandum on a Conversation between Greek Defence Minister and the Italian Ambassador, 25 September 1974". The Italian Ambassador visited Averof on behalf of the Italian Minister Aldo Moro who wanted to brief the Greek government about his meeting with the Turkish Foreign Minister.

3 Averof Archive: Folder 31: "Averof's Brief Memorandum on his Conversation with Abdel Aziz Mohamed Hegazy, 13 September 1974".

4 NATO archive: Document C-R (74) 60 PD: "Summary Record of a Meeting Held at the Headquarters of NATO in Brussels on 12 and 13 December 1974".

5 Cyprus State Archive: Folder FA 2/103: "Notes by the Attorney-General of the Republic on the Agreement Reached between Archbishop Makarios and Mr. Denktas, 12 February 1977".

6 NATO Confidential: Folder PO/82/138: "Secretary General's Report on his Watching Brief to the December 1982 Ministerial Meeting"; State Archive of Israel: 8940/6 "Israel-Cyprus-Greece Relations 30 January 1982, Repost about the Trip of US Congressman (Democrat) Benjamin Rosenthal to the Eastern Mediterranean".

7 State Archive of Israel: 8940/6: "Israel-Cyprus-Greece Relations 30 January 1982, Repost about the Trip of US Congressman (Democrat) Benjamin Rosenthal to the Eastern Mediterranean".

8 CIA Releases 2017: "Directorate of Intelligence, a Contingency Study on a Greek-Turkish Military Confrontation 9 June 1983".

9 PRO: FCO 9/4648: "Telegram of the British Embassy in Athens to the Foreign Office and the Diplomatic Authorities in Ankara, Nicosia, Washington 23 February 1984"; "Telegram from the British Embassy in Athens to the Foreign Office in London and the British Embassies around the World, 17 April 1984".

10 The British were worried that the new provision would affect British citizens living in the "TRNC" as well. In general, travellers who had been previously in TRNC encountered problems with the immigration authorities in Greece. It seems that the British regarded this policy as very worrisome and contemplated to issue second passports for some persons. PRO: FCO 9/4648:

"Exchange of Letters between the British Embassy in Athens, Istanbul and Foreign Office in London in March, April, May and June 1984".

11 On 18 April 1984, representatives of the NATO embassies in Athens were summoned in the Greek Foreign Ministry, at which they were briefed by the Greek government on Turkey's latest action, which was labelled as brutal and unacceptable act and opposing to the views of the international Community. PRO: FCO 9/4648: "Telegram from the British Embassy in Athens to the Foreign Office in London and the British Embassies around the World, 18 April 1984".

12 Denktash's intransigent stance in the overall negotiations process to find a comprehensive solution of the Cyprus Problem is confirmed by the US ambassador in Ankara 1977–1980 Ronald I. Spiers:

13 PRO: FCO 9/4648: "Telegram titled *Greece-Cyprus-Turkey* from the British Embassy in Ankara to the British diplomatic authorities in Istanbul, Athens and London 15 April 1984".

14 PRO: FCO 9/4648: "Confidential Telegram from the British Embassy in Ankara to the British diplomatic authorities in Athens, Nicosia, Washington et al. 3 April 1984".

15 PRO: FCO 9/4648: "Internal Report of the Foreign Office on the Upcoming Anglo-US Political and Military Talks on the 12 April 1984 on the Subject: Southern Flank Issues; Greece and Turkey (ii) 6 April 1984".

16 PRO: FCO 9/4648: "Confidential Telegram from the British Embassy in Ankara 15 March 1984".

17 PRO: FCO 9/4648: "Exchange of Telegrams and Letters between the British Diplomatic Authorities in Athens, Ankara London, NATO and Nicosia in May and June 1984".

18 US Department of State Releases 2017: "Bureau of International Security and Non-Proliferation. Document of the Stockholm Conference on Confidence- and Security-Building Measures and Disarmament in Europe Convened in Accordance with the Relevant Provisions of the Concluding Document of the Madrid Meeting of the Conference on Security and Cooperation in Europe (CSBMs) Signed at Stockholm September 19, 1986".

19 NATO Archive: Document IMSWM-ENG-125–88: "Memorandum for all Members of the Military Committee, Subject: Military Review of the Document of the Stockholm Conference in Light of the First Year of Implementation, 10 June 1988".

References

Primary sources

Cyprus State Archives (Archive of Foreign Ministry)
Public Record Office (PRO)
State Archive of Israel
US Department of State Releases
CIA Releases
NATO Archive

Secondary sources

Bahcheli, T. 1989. *Greek-Turkish Relations since 1955*. San Francisco and London: Westview Press.

Balkir, C., & Yalma, G., 2009. Economics and the politisation of civil society: The Turkish-Cypriot case. In Th. Diez and N. Tocci (eds.), *Cyprus a conflict at the crossroads* (pp. 48–65). Manchester and New York: Manchester University Press.

Dodd, C., 2010. *The History and Politics of the Cyprus Conflict*. Basingstoke, Hampshire: Palgrave-Macmillan.

Féron, E., & Lisaniler, F. G., 2009. The Cyprus conflict in a comparative perspective: assessing the impact of European integration. In: Th. Dietz & N. Tocci (eds.), *Cyprus: A Conflict at the Crossroads*. (1st ed.) (pp. 198–216). Manchester and New York: Manchester University Press.

Joseph, J., 2005. Post-colonial period, 1960–1974: Expectations and failures. In M. Michael, and A. Tamis (eds.), *Cyprus in the Modern World* (pp. 25–56). Thessaloniki: Vanias.

Kizilyürek, N., 2005. The Turkish Cypriot community and rethinking of Cyprus. In M. Michael, and A. Tamis (eds), *Cyprus in the Modern World* (pp. 228–247). Thessaloniki: Vanias.

Kranidiotis, Y., 1992. Relations between Cyprus and the European Community. *Modern Greek Studies Yearbook*, vol. 8, 165–206.

Loizides, N., 2007. Ethnic nationalism and adaptation in Cyprus. *International Studies Perspectives*, 8, 172–189.

Papapolyviou, P., 2021. Mia Apopeira Katagrafis tis istorias tis Kypriakis Dimokratias meta to 1974 [An attempt to round up the history of the Republic Cyprus after 1974]. In A. Aimiliniades, C. Ioannou and D. Sotiropoulos (eds.), *Agonas gia epiviosi. Ptiches tis kipriakis politikis istorias meta to 1974 [Struggle for Survival. Aspects of Cypriot Political History after 1974]*. Nicosia: Hippasus Publishing, pp. 11–23.

Richter, H. 2021. *The conflicts of the Aegean in the 20th century*. Peleus Studien zur Geschichte Griechenlands und Zyperns Band 113. Wiesbaden: Harrassowitz Verlag.

Rumelili, B., 2008. Transforming the Greek-Turkish conflicts: The EU and "what we make of it". In Th. Diez, St. Stetter, and M. Albert (eds.), *The European Union and Border Conflicts* (pp. 94–128). Cambridge: Cambridge University Press.

Stergiou, A., 2012. *Kypriako. H Lysi ton dyo kraton. To germaniko paradigma [The Cyprus Problem: A Solution Through Two States. The German Paradigm]*. Athens: Tourikis Publisher.

Stergiou, A., 2015. Greek–Israeli Defense and Energy Ties: Writing a New Chapter in Bilateral Relations, *Israel Journal of Foreign Affairs*, 9 (3), 417–428.

Stergiou, A. 2023. Economy of Cyprus until 2022. In J. O'Brien (ed.), *The Middle East and North Africa 2023*. (69th ed.) (pp. 129–138). London and New York: Routledge.

Tzermias, P., 1998. *Geschichte der Republic Zypern* (3rd ed.). Tübingen: Francke Verlag.

5 Greek–Turkish relations in the 1980s

The 1980s in Greece are interwoven with the Panhellenic Socialist Movement (PASOK) administration that began in 1981 and lasted through the whole decade. The PASOK's rise to power coincided with the flare-up of the Cold War all over the world and especially the spread of the fear of a limited nuclear war in Europe. In the era of the PASOK administration, Greece's relations with NATO and Turkey were seriously tested. Whilst in opposition the unquestionable charismatic leader of the PASOK Andreas Papandreou had insisted that the US, NATO and the "West" were the causes of the "Greek tragedy" and had put the struggle against these forces at the top of his political priorities. Furthermore, the PASOK accused the West of pressing the previous Greek conservative governments to engage in negotiations with Turkey in order to serve NATO's regional objectives,[1] at the expense of the country's national interests. Papandreou also criticised the conciliatory negotiation policy of his predecessor, Karamanlis, as an indication of weakness and lack of resolve (Coufoudakis, 1993, pp. 167–180).

Upon taking over the post of the Prime Minister of Greece in October 1981, Papandreou informed NATO allies that the danger to Greek security came primarily from Turkey and secondarily from the Soviet Bloc. Therefore, NATO should extend a security guarantee for Greece's frontier against potential Turkish aggression. Nevertheless, in December 1981, at the meeting of NATO countries' Defence Ministers, he demanded that the alliance members acknowledge the Turkish aggression, but he met a categorical denial. In response and in a demonstration of the new foreign policy style, Greece blocked the signing of the NATO Joint Communique for the first time in the history of the organisation (Papacosma, 2001, pp. 365–366).

This was the first sign of a series of deeds, unmistakably highlighting Greek Socialists' attitude to NATO. In the next years, Athens

DOI: 10.4324/9781003350033-6

did not hesitate to obstruct NATO military business (infrastructure projects, military exercises and so on), raising concerns that it may systematically mess things up on the military side of NATO preparing the ground for some grand gesture or act of defiance against the alliance. For instance, Papandreou linked his approval of various NATO infrastructure projects on the condition that the alliance prioritise the financing of projects of Greek interest. He also put down a marker about unfunded Greek projects of previous years. These were basically projects funded nationally by the Greeks, whilst they were outside the integrated military structure but continuing to pay their contributions to the infrastructure budget (Stergiou, 2021, p. 142).

The most striking appraisal of the PASOK's foreign policy in that period emanates from a report of the British embassy in Greece. According to the British diplomats, the Papandreou government, partly from natural disposition, partly for reasons of domestic politics and partly because of the benefits it believed this could bring to the country's international position, was pursuing a foreign policy which was consciously and deliberately "independent" of that followed by other members of the NATO alliance. The fact that this policy was not only on occasion embarrassing to other allies but also damaging to alliance solidarity appeared to be of little or no concern to the Greek socialists. Yet, despite the anti-NATO noises made by Papandreou during the election campaign, he showed every sign of wishing to keep Greece in the alliance and to continue to enjoy the benefits membership brings to his government. Papandreou, so the British appraisal went, was realistic enough to know that to leave NATO would run a very serious risk of forfeiting American military support, a consequence which would be a disaster for his government and for Greece's ability to meet the perceived threat from Turkey. But Papandreou also knew that the other allies were sufficiently aware of the damage which Greece's withdrawal would do to the alliance (especially in political terms, but also militarily given Greece's geographical position on the alliance's already very weak south-eastern flank) and therefore it could not afford to drive Greece out.[2]

Moreover, assuming office in October 1981, Papandreou broke off talks with the Turks making it clear that he was in no hurry to resume dialogue with Ankara, especially since he issued a public statement, that Greece faced a threat against its sovereignty by another member state of the alliance. Turkey reacted angrily accusing Athens of trying to reverse the provisions of the *Roger Plan*. It was the advent of a very difficult co-existence of the two states in the same alliance. Even NATO's Secretary General acknowledged with some regret in his annual report on Greek–Turkish relations by the end of 1981 that the progress in the Greek–Turkish dialogue that had begun in 1980 with a view to narrowing their differences, had not yet developed to the hoped-for extent.[3] In his watching brief of 1982, the NATO Secretary General's assessment of the relations between Greece and Turkey was even more pessimistic. Not only did the relationship remain under strain, annulling the optimism deriving from Greece's re-integration into the military structure of NATO, but things appeared to get worse. The cancellation of the meeting of Foreign Ministers planned for December 1982 was a particular cause for disappointment.[4]

After a gesture of goodwill by Turkish Prime Minister Özal in the spring of 1983 that was characterised as an "olive branch", a dialogue between senior officials covering only economic issues was resumed in July 1983. After only one meeting, this dialogue also was broken off in response to the TRNC's declaration of independence which added another serious twist to an already tense relationship.[5] This bumpy course is reflected in the December 1983 assessment of NATO Secretary General, Joseph Luns. From the state of optimism to which he stood after the constructive meeting between the Greek and Turkish Foreign Ministers at Strasbourg in April 1983, at which both parties expressed the willingness of their governments to increase the efforts made with a view to improving relations and a later meeting in Ankara that produced an agreed intention to work together on certain economic and tourism questions, he quickly relapsed to a state of pessimism. As a matter of fact, a fresh start seemed to be underway. A new dialogue process was initiated which could eventually result in real progress towards the resolution of differences between the two countries. Continuing disagreements over command-and-control arrangements and operational responsibilities in the Aegean and the developments in Cyprus, however, not only hampered efforts to establish an allied command headquarters at Larissa (Greece), but also posed serious problems for essential NATO exercises in the region.[6]

In the CIA's judgment, Papandreou's hard-line policy on Turkey and the Aegean, which differed more in tone than in substance from that of his predecessors aimed at eliciting army's loyalty and "to strike a responsive chord among military officers" who saw Turkey as a growing regional power with ambitions on Greek territory.[7]

It is noteworthy that even members of the opposing alliance, the Warsaw Pact, such as the East Germans estimated that after the take-over of power by Papandreou and the radicalisation of his rhetoric, especially his castigation of the *Roger Plan* as an act of surrendering sovereign rights to Turkey, the danger of a conflict between Greece and Turkey had aggravated. Contrary to Karamanlis, who was ready to discuss the control of the airspace over the Aegean with Ankara, the assessment went, Papandreou evaluated this question as more important than the question of the continental shelf and he appeared not willing to approve of the *Roger Plan*, unless NATO the operational boundaries finalised. According to the East Germans, the repeated violations of the Greek air sovereignty in early 1982 by Turkish fighter planes in response to the research activities for oil east of the island Thassos, were connived by the United States and NATO in order to show Papandreou his limits and to compel him to accept the Roger plan.[8]

On the other hand, Papandreou overtly questioned fundamental NATO policies at this point in time like the so-called double-track decision, notably aimed at containing the deployment of the Soviet intermediate-range nuclear forces in Europe, arguing instead for disarmament. Since this issue was highly sensitive for Germany, this topic was quite hotly debated between Athens and Bonn in the early 1980s.[9] Papandreou also complained to his NATO, especially the Americans, partners that Greece was discriminated against in comparison to Turkey in the delivery of weaponry. This might be the reason why the PASOK administration partially diversified the country's arms suppliers in favour of European countries, a shift that gradually led to a decline in the almost monopolistic position of US-based arms producers in the Greek market (Stergiou & Kollias, 2018). Federal Germany got a big chunk of the new orders.[10]

Athens also tried through the Greek lobby to influence US congressional attitude on military assistance to Turkey. Ankara, on its turn, also tried to influence US Congress to the favour of Turkish security interests, as there was the rumour that Athens had obtained an implicit concession from the Americans on the so-called 7 to 10 ratio, which, however, was denied by the Americans. For the fiscal year 1985, the US Administration asked Congress for $500 million of military aid for Greece and $755 million for Turkey. Congressional committees recommended that the figure for Turkey should be reduced to $716 million (thus restoring the 7 to 10 ratio) and to Turkey's dismay, linking it, as it has already been mentioned, to the handover of Varosha to UN control.[11]

In February 1984, Papandreou publicly accused Turkey of raising claims on Greek territory, repeated his refusal to negotiate on Greece's sovereign rights, called for pressure on Turkey over Cyprus and reiterated his criticism of US military aid. He brought up once again the argument that the air defence boundary could not be moved west-wards because this would place some Greek islands under the protection of the Turkish air force. In the case of the militarisation of Lemnos (an apple of contention between Turkey and Greece), he accused Turkey of attempting to use legal obstacles to put constraints on Greek sovereignty. Greece was allegedly ready to use similar legal obstacles against Turkey.[12]

An incident in the Aegean Sea on 8 March 1984 further soured the bilateral relations. The Greeks accused Turkish vessels of firing close to a Greek destroyer named Panther and Greek fishing vessels and ordered the recall of their Ambassador from Ankara. But the incident subsided when it became clear that the Turks had not intended any provocation and the Greek ship was closer to the exercise zone than where it should have been. Greece's Ambassador recall was also cancelled.[13]

The flurry in the Aegean was refuelled by hardliners on both sides. High-rank officials in the Turkish Foreign Ministry alleged that the history of the past 150 years had been one of Greek expansionism eastward with western connivance and as late as the 1930s there were British plans to hand over part of Turkey to the Italians. They also alleged that the risk of further action by Greece to extend territorial limits was very likely, most probably coupled with military enforcement to the Greek troops in Cyprus. Turkey would have no option but to undertake reciprocal military action to restore the military balance. Much of the current trouble "had been stirred up by the Greek Communist party with Soviet instigation, as the extension of the territorial waters suited the Soviets"![14]

By the end of March 1984, the Greek government repeatedly protested to the Turkish Ambassador in Greece against violations of Greek airspace and territorial waters during the so-called Turkish Sea Wolf exercises in the Aegean. Athens also claimed that Turkish naval aircraft and a helicopter had violated Greek airspace on six occasions, whilst between 24 and 26 March Turkish naval vessels had entered Greek waters in the area of Rhodes without navigation lights thereby infringing the rules of safe passage.[15]

In May 1984, Athens complained to its NATO allies that Turkey, a signatory member of the Montreux Convention on the straits, had issued in 1982 a statistical pamphlet on navigation in the straits using Turkish names for a number of Greek islands and mainland cities.[16] Ankara on the contrary, complained that the Turkish national airspace had been violated by Greek fighter aircraft. This was vehemently denied by Athens. Ankara also complained about Papandreou's "incendiary" rhetoric and anti-Turkish statements.[17] At the same time, Athens objected to the deployment of the harpoon missile defence systems along Turkey's Aegean coast under the auspices of NATO as contrary to Greece's security. The move was then presented as a "bold and courageous gambit" and an indication of the "new national independent" foreign policy at the party Congress of PASOK as a "rally party members around the flag" method.[18]

Furthermore, in June 1984, the *New York Times* revealed that Greece sought to reverse NATO's approval of Turkish plans for developing its armed forces which included procurement of modernised missiles for use against shipping. It was the first time that one ally attempted to stop another from improving its forces (Vinocur, 1984).

The stand of the relations between the two neighbour allies became gradually so worrisome for the coherence of the alliance that the Southern European Department of the Foreign Office started working on contingency plans on the basis of the hypothetical scenario of an incident in the Aegean Sea leading to an escalation of tension between Greece and Turkey.[19]

The fortification (or the militarisation) of the Aegean islands (Limnos, Samothrace, Mytilene, Chios, Samos and Ikaria, and the Dodecanese islands: Stampalia, Rhodes, Calki, Scarpanto, Casos, Piscopis, Nisiros, Calimnos, Leros, Patmos, Lipsos, Symi, Cos and Castellorizo), to which Athens resorted at the same time, additionally burdened the Greek–Turkish relations causing a serious headache to NATO.

The inclusion of Lemnos island into the NATO exercises had seriously disrupted NATO operations in the region for quite some time. Turkey had been seeking since 1965 the exclusion of Lemnos, the Samothrace and Agios Efstratios islands from NATO's military planning, claiming that these islands should be demilitarised according to the *Treaty of Lausanne*. In 1978, the alliance's legal adviser, Bayle rejected these arguments and opined in favour of Lemnos inclusion into NATO military planning. In 1979, however, during the negotiations on Greece's re-integration into NATO, SACEUR's position on the same issue was, allegedly based on military criteria, in favour of Turkey's demands. Later, NATO Secretary General Luns, suggested the exclusion of Lemnos from defence infrastructure and equipment programmes of allied funding as a means to defuse the row. Since 1982, Greece refused to participate in NATO exercises planned and carried out in the Aegean which did not engulf Lemnos (Roubatis, 1986, pp. 93–113).

In 1983 and 1984 an array of NATO exercises (Wintex, Distant Drum, Adventure Express, Display Determination, Distant Hammer) were disrupted due to Greece's insistence that Lemnos be included in NATO exercises set against NATO's policy of excluding exercises in areas of dispute between partners. The Foreign Office felt compelled to work out a report on the legal background of the dispute.[20] In this report, the British experts appear to adopt the Greek argument that the replacement of the Lausanne Convention by the Montreux Convention 1936 led to the abrogation of the demilitarisation provisions for the islands Lemnos and Samothraki as was the case with the Bosporus Straits, although the Turks had avoided a complete remilitarisation of the islands Imbros, Tenedos and the Rabit islands that were also located in the same area. The Turks, according to the report, first reacted to the remilitarisation of Lemnos in 1970 but the strength of their protest increased after 1974 probably because of Greece's withdrawal from NATO Integrated Military Structure. Their arguments were based firstly on the absence of specific mention in the Montreux Convention of Lemnos and Samothrace and therefore the absence of expressed permission to Greece to remilitarise these islands. The Turks also referred to Article 12 of the *Treaty of Lausanne* (1923) and the decision by the six powers in February 1914 following the *Treaty of London* (1913), according to which the six powers granted sovereignty of certain Aegean islands (including Lemnos) to Greece on the condition that those islands would remain demilitarised. Greece had accepted it and this principle was accepted by all at Lausanne. In line with the British legal interpretation, neither argument is sound. The first can be dismissed on the grounds that the travaux of the Montreux Convention clearly demonstrate that the intention was that Lemnos and Samothrace could be remilitarised and this was admitted by the Turkish Minister as well. The second argument can be dismissed on the grounds that the Greeks acceded to the six powers' decision on the condition that Turkey would act likewise in the Imbros and Tenedos islands. Turkey did not accept the decision and the question was unresolved when World War II broke out. Moreover, whilst Article 12 of the *Treaty of Lausanne* did confirm the Lausanne decision, the confirmation only went as far as sovereignty, not demilitarisation. Further, Article 13, requiring Greece to maintain only nominal military forces on four islands, did not include Lemnos.[21]

In 1984, Athens began upgrading the fortification of the Aegean islands. In the so-called South-West Asia Impact Report from 1983, NATO commanders had backed the idea of militarising the Aegean islands as regions to be defended should an invasion not be confined at the Bosphorus Straits but Greek–Turkish tensions prevented a formal approval of the report.[22]

Against this background, Athens purported that the fortification served NATO interests. More precisely, it extended the strategic depth of north-eastern Greece and hence of NATO against a Warsaw Pact threat, thereby posing a formidable obstacle for the free movement of hostile ships to and from Dardanelles and a deterrent against the Soviet fleet. Athens further argued that the undertaking was designed to resist a Soviet attempt to occupy and transform the islands into naval bases. The island Karpathos, in particular, was presented as a likely objective of Soviet strategy. The construction of new airfields on the various islands was justified as offering Greek pilots full control over the Aegean Sea. In the case of an East–West confrontation, the success of Soviet naval operations in the Mediterranean, the argument went, would largely depend on the support received by backfire bombers taking off from Crimean airfields. A partial defence against their effectiveness could be the network of Greek radars located on various strategically located Aegean islands. Furthermore, the Limnos airfield could provide full air support to land operations in Thrace, and that island, along with Samothrace and Lesvos, formed the first of a succession of choke points to hinder the passage of the Soviet fleet in the area. If the Soviet Escadra circulating in the Aegean or eastern Mediterranean attempted to aid Warsaw Pact forces in Thracian land operations, these islands could form the last choke point for denying the Soviets access to their destination (Veremis, 1993, p. 184).

Expectably, these arguments were not enough to assuage Ankara which immediately reacted against Athens' actions, demanding NATO not to operate in alliance territory which was in dispute between Greece and Turkey. When, in May 1984, the NATO CINCSOUTH Admiral Small told the Turkish press that the airstrip and the radar in Lemnos islands, operated by the 88th support force, was legitimate, justified in terms of Greece's defence requirements and also had been offered for NATO use, drew critical comments by the Turkish military authorities. Even the British Ambassador in Ankara opined that Admiral Small stepped out of line and straight to "one of the more political sensitive aspects of the nexus of the Turco-Greek disputes".[23]

Ankara was also infuriated by the chapter of the NATO defence review, published that year, referring to Greece and in particular to Lemnos as well as by Athens' insistence to include the militarisation of Lemnos in NATO documents. That, in Turkey's opinion, would pave the way for the militarisation of other islands too including Dodecanes. NATO authorities had to rewrite the chapters on Turkey and Greece again and again until the two countries were satisfied.[24]

The argument the Turks usually came up with against the militar-isation of the eastern Aegean islands was that in 1969 Greece had officially assured the Turks that they were bound by the *Lausanne Treaty* obligations and were not militarising the islands, through this had gone on since 1964, was, according to Ankara, a hallmark of the continuing legal validity of the treaty. Turkey had allegedly prevented the Greeks from installing troops on Lemnos at the last minute.[25]

In order to justify the presence of the Aegean Army, notably sta-tioned at the coast of the Asia Minor across the Greek islands, Turkey used the same arguments, as Greece did with the fortification of the eastern Aegean islands. The Turkish militaries purported that "the main job of this peace-time army was training" and that Athens' and Nicosia's reactions were not serious. In the words of a Turkish Gen-eral ... *anything more would be intolerable, not just to Turkey, but, for example, to the Soviet Union and to other major powers. It was "essential" with the chaos in Lebanon, Iran, Iraq etc that Greece and Turkey should preserve an area of stability, particularly as they were NATO allies ... The only beneficiary of a conflict between Greece and Turkey would be the Soviet Union.* [26]

The Greek socialist administration perceived NATO's unwillingness to resolve the Lemnos dispute as a clear partisan and pro-Turkish stance. On the same trajectory, the British government's refusal to take an authoritative position on the issue under the pretext of not taking sides was seen by the Greeks as in fact siding with Turkey. London's inaction, however, incurred the distrust of Turkey as well, as the latter regarded the British as unreliable. On the other hand, the British believed that neither side was genuinely interested in resolving the dispute. So, any arrangement which would improve the situation would probably be seen by both sides as demanding from them a too great concession. If the objective were to resolve the dispute, the legal status of Lemnos should be separated from the other issues in the Aegean. Since the British government had little influence on both sides, any initiative would be considered as partisan. The US had the weight to move things forward but was viewed askance by Athens at that certain time.[27]

The issue seriously preoccupied the British and Americans. They were concerned especially about Turkey's reactions as a factor dama-ging the unity of the alliance but also Anglo–Turkish and American–Turkish relations. There were intense deliberations on how to solve the problem without alienating any of the two countries. NATO General Secretary Lord Carrington also stepped in in order to defuse the situation and calm Turkey but in vain.[28]

In April 1984, the British realised that they had been embroiled in the labyrinthine disputes between Turkey and Greece over the status of the Greek islands in the eastern Aegean, the delineation of the continental shelf, territorial waters, territorial airspace and airspace questions, and these affected their interests. Therefore, in the next months, the Foreign Office officials began contemplating potential solutions to the problem. One of them was that the Greeks would stop insisting on including Lemnos in future NATO drills in exchange for the Turks secretly accepting the remilitarisation of Lemnos with the *Montreux Treaty*. However, this scenario had a few snugs: Ankara would suspect that Papandreou would leak the private agreement when he judged it advantageous. Athens, for its part, would argue that only the inclusion of Lemnos into the NATO exercises would give substance to the assurance that Lemnos would be defended by the alliance if attacked. A more realistic quid pro quo for the Turks accepting the de-demilitarised status of Lemnos island would be for the Greeks to limit their airspace claim to 6 miles and cease requiring notification of military flights within their FIR.[29]

Offering the Turks and possibly the Greeks the perspective that the British believed the Greeks were violating Article 13 of the *Treaty of Lausanne* and Article 41 of the *Treaty of Paris* (1947) by militarising the Mytilene group of islands and the Dodecanese islands was another counterbalance the British considered making to the Turks. This would precipitate the withdrawal of Greek forces from Samos, Chios and Rhodos. The Greeks would counter that such a move would upset the military balance in the Aegean and necessitate the reduction of Turkey's Aegean army, so it was feared that the Turks would immediately exert pressure on the British to demand that the Greeks demilitarise the islands. The same report notes that the Greeks appeared to have a stronger legal position, despite the British perspective on the demilitarisation of various Greek islands. However, the Greeks were considered to be unreliable. They recently leveraged the disagreement to abruptly cancel a NATO exercise. Further, if the British made their view public, the Greeks would immediately publicise it to their own benefit without showing any gratitude. As a result, London had been careful not to take sides. Publicly, it only regretted every cancellation of NATO exercises and declared support of a solution to the dispute through dialogue and not through a pronouncement by Her Majesty's Government on legal issues.[30]

This was the British attitude in the years that followed, as the problem continued to cause issues within the alliance. Since the British had recognised in 1937 Greece's right to remilitarise Lemnos, they were beleaguered by the Greek Foreign Ministry to take a more assertive position on the matter. For this reason, British diplomats were instructed in November 1987 to downplay the relevance of 1937 papers and to resist being drawn into the dispute about Lemnos by arguing that events had moved on and Greece and Turkey were in the same alliance now. They also should emphasise that the British concern was with NATO solidarity and not with taking sides.[31]

The Greek–Turkish antagonism was salient at another level as well. During the 1980s, Greece and Turkey lobbied against each other bitterly in Brussels and in Washington and often used the same arguments to disrupt NATO's allocation of infrastructure funds. NATO repeatedly undertook determined efforts to resolve the differences. However, this was all in vain. As an experienced US diplomat, who also served in Greece, pointed out, in 1987 and 1988 Athens' and Ankara's objections to specific projects proposed for infrastructure funding on each other's territory prohibited the approval of about half of the projects whose disbursement required unanimous consent. Turkey lost $252 million and Greece $144 million. The disputed projects were located in areas, including the Greek island of Limnos and the Turkish coastline adjacent to it that were essential to NATO's defence of the straits of the Dardanelles but would be equally significant in the event of Greek–Turkish hostilities. The Greek–Turkish rivalry also affected common exercises conducted by NATO (Stearns, 1992, pp. 68–71).

In January 1985, Athens officially announced its new defence doctrine that clearly directed the deterrent attention of its armed forces to Turkey rather than to the Northern Communist countries. A few months later, in March 1985, Andreas Papandreou announced the ambitious for the then Greek standards purchase of 80 fighter aircraft, 40 F-16 and 40 Mirage 2000, which was called the purchase of the century (Kollias, 1995). At the same time, Turkey also proceeded into major defence contracts with the United Kingdom and West Germany, especially as Turkey was interested in modernising its air defence systems.[32]

Once again, the Foreign Office felt compelled to prepare contingency plans for a possible incident in the Aegean. Two possible incidents were regarded as very likely: a) a clash between Greek and Turkish ships or aircraft in disputed waters and airspace, and b) a less likely scenario for conflict, mineral exploration (most probably by Turkey) on the disputed continental shelf. Several measures were suggested such as urging restraint on both sides, through bilateral channels; encouraging other influential countries to do the same;

summoning ambassadors; dispatching of UN observer or peace-keeping force, etc.[33]

In 1986, Greece and Turkey constantly quarrelled over airspace violations. Athens repeatedly informed NATO authorities of the infringement of the Athens FIR by Turkish aircraft. Athens also protested to NATO regarding non-compliance with Greek Civil aviation instructions during exercise display determination.[34]

As horrified CIA officials noted in September 1986,[35] several factors suggested that the situation this time was worsening in subtle and potentially dangerous ways. Turkey appeared to be adopting a tougher policy towards Greece as suggested by Turkish Prime Minister Özal's public statements about the limits of Turkish patience. Likewise, Papandreou had gone "beyond previous limits in his warning that any attempt to expand the Turkish occupation in Cyprus would lead to open conflict".[36]

The prolonged crisis in Greek–Turkish relations led to a culmination in early 1987 conforming to British estimations about the nature of a possible clash between the two countries. At the beginning of February 1987, the international oil consortium North Aegean Petroleum Company announced that it was planning to drill east of the Greek island Thasos. Out of fear of a possible confrontation with Turkey, the Greek government passed a law with a view of becoming a shareholder of the company and thus determining the company's course. On the same day (27 February), the Turkish Ambassador in Athens, Nazmi Akiman, lodged an official protest demanding Greece to "respect the Berne Declaration" (the 1976 agreement according to which the two states pledged to *refrain from any initiative or act concerning the Aegean continental shelf*). In Ankara, the acting Prime Minister Erdem (Turkey's elected Prime Minister Özal was in the US for medical treatment) stated that drilling within 10 nautical miles of Thasos violated the Berne Declaration. Athens rejected Ankara's accusations as legally unfounded calling on Turkey to submit the case to the International Court of Justice. In Athens' official statement the Berne Declaration had become inoperative with Turkey's breaking off of negotiations in September 1981. In March 1987, the Canadian-controlled oil company that had made the Thassos oil find in Northern Greece announced that it would drill in an area outside Greek territorial waters claimed by Turkey. Subsequently, Ankara asserted that the entire Aegean Sea outside the respective territorial waters was "disputed territory", thereby accusing Greece of expansionist plans. Soon after, the Turkish ship Piri Reis accompanied by two warships started carrying out research without informing Athens in an area in which Greece had its own territory. Simultaneously, it became known that the Turkish government had granted the Turkish state oil company TPAO exploration and drilling licences in the Aegean Sea near Samothrace, Limnos and Lesvos. On 27 March, Papandreou briefed the full cabinet in detail on the situation heralding a tough response against Turkey. Papandreou also stressed that if this was an attempt by NATO or the US to force Greece to negotiate with Turkey on all issues, the Greek government would not accept it and would inform the Bulgarian government, i.e. a member of the Warsaw Pact, in accordance with the existing non-aggression pact between the two countries, about Greece's intentions. Should a conflict arise, the US bases in Greece would also be closed. Moreover, the Greek Foreign Minister Papoulias decided to brief first the ambassadors of the Warsaw Pact countries and the Islamic countries on the situation and only afterwards the NATO countries, which caused considerable irritation in NATO circles. In Ankara, a military spokesperson announced that the research ship would leave for the Aegean the following day under military protection and if this were obstructed, countermeasures would be taken without hesitation. The Turkish armed forces along the Evros border, the Aegean coast and in Northern Cyprus were put on alert (Richter, 2021, pp. 46–55).

Washington, London and NATO were mobilised to avert the looming war putting the Turkish government under pressure. The war was averted literally at the very last moment after the resolute intervention by NATO Secretary General to the Greek and Turkish Prime Ministers and a subsequent call conversation between Papandreou and Özal. On 28 March, the de-escalation process was initiated, as the Piri Reis returned to the Turkish territorial waters without military escort and the North Aegean Petroleum Company announced that it would refrain from drilling outside Greek territorial waters (Rizas, 2000, pp. 91–97).

Foreign intervention was indeed of paramount importance for the aversion to war. Swifts in the international context seem to explain why an external factor was more successful in this and confirm what American diplomats later admitted, that the reluctance of the United States and NATO to be distracted from their principal mission of Soviet containment by political differences within the alliance had enabled the emergence of so much friction in Greek–Turkish relations (Stergiou, 2021, pp. 80–82). Accumulated information from intelligence collectors co-operated with surface combatants in the surveillance of NATO forces at sea and established intelligence collection patrols off Naples, south of the Turkish littoral, off the coast of Israel, and in the Aegean Sea indicated that the Soviet naval presence in the Mediterranean (SOVMEDRON) at that point of time was maintained at the low levels and was expected to remain so. Current SOVME-DRON levels may have been sufficient to monitor the movements of NATO forces and to "show the flag" throughout the Mediterranean in support of Soviet foreign policy. However, If the need would arise, SOVMEDRON should be reinforced by surface and air units from the Black Sea. In view of the terms of the Montreux Convention, Soviet submarines had, however, to make long transits from their Northern or Baltic Fleet bases. Moreover, the Soviets had no nuclear submarines in their Black Sea fleet and the number of conventional units assigned to the fleet left little reserve for operations outside the area.[37] The decrease of the Soviet threat in the crucial period left the necessary space for the stronger NATO countries to deal with the Greek–Turkish rivalry more effectively.

The British embassy in Athens received through private channels with state officials the information that the crisis had been handled exclusively by Papandreou and the Ministers Papoulias and Kapsis by cutting out the permanent diplomats. Kapsis shall have contributed to the outbreak of the crisis with his actions.[38]

In the following months, Papandreou and Özal tried to keep the issue out of the public arena. Mainly to avoid criticism from the domestic opposition. Ahead of the constitutional referendum of September 1987 in Turkey aimed at amending the "temporary Article" 4 of the constitution, which had forbidden the leaders of banned parties from taking part in politics for ten years, the Turks wanted to avoid any controversy. There were written exchanges between the two leaders, whose content was kept secret, since the official positions remained unchanged. Greece was pushing for a joint recourse to the International Court in The Hague, whilst Turkey insisted that the dialogue should be political and broadly based and that recourse should be the last resort. Nevertheless, the British embassy registered "a guarded optimism in the air".[39]

Subsequently, in January 1988, at a meeting of the World Economic Forum in Davos, Switzerland, Papandreou and Özal forged a "no-war agreement", also inaugurating a comprehensive dialogue covering all the issues in the Greek–Turkish relations. The two leaders also made public their intention to proceed with military confidence-building measures. This was a watershed in PASOK's Greek foreign policy, since Papandreou, as Karamanlis had done in the 1970s, agreed for the very first time to discuss other issues except the delineation of the continental shelf. More precisely, the joint communique stated that ...

The two Prime Ministers observed that the problems which had accumulated with the passage of time were due to the operation of different approaches and had become the object of exploitation by certain circles; the two Prime Ministers presented their views on Greek–Turkish relations, as approached from "a historical perspective" (in this regard new schoolbooks should be written); both sides ought to direct their efforts "towards the creation of permanent peaceful relations"; a rapprochement between the two countries "would demand decisiveness. constant efforts and the development of trust"; two committees would be set up assigned with the tasks of "an examination of the areas within which problems existed and of an examination of the prospects for a bridging of the hiatus and for a movement towards permanent solutions" (Lioliou, 1999, pp. 186–187).

The agreement was followed by what was labelled as the "spirit of Davos", meaning a series of agreements on "low politics" issues (tourism, economy, education and culture) as well as certain gestures of goodwill by both sides (Tsardanidis, 2002, p. 244).

In the realm of the Davos Declaration two committees were established, one of a political nature and headed by the Foreign Ministers, having been tasked to draw up a list of issues on which Greece and Turkey had bilateral differences and, in the longer term, to try to solve those differences. However, ten months later it was still not possible even to prepare such a list. On the contrary, in the deliberations for NATO common-funded infrastructure programme for the year 1988, Turkey refused to consent to the installation of a tactical air navigation system which was used by military aircraft on the Greek island of Rhodes with the excuse that the respective island was under a demilitarised status. In response, Greece placed a reservation on all NATO projects that should be realised in Turkey by claiming that Turkey had no legal right to make any claims with regard to the status of the Dodecanese islands. Further, it was claimed that the navigation system was operated and maintained by members of the internal security personnel stationed in Rhodes in accordance with the definition of the demilitarisation terms of the *Paris Treaty.* [40]

Within NATO, the United Kingdom expressed its disappointment that agreement on an infrastructure slice had again been blocked by a dispute between two allies. This was a problem which would have to be solved by Greece and by Turkey alone and not by the alliance.[41]

Some scholars have argued that the strain of significant military spending on Greece's already precarious balance of payments and the protracted period of mandatory military service, which hurt the government's populist image, persuaded Andreas Papandreou to raise the bar for a possible war between Greece and Turkey (Veremis, 1993, p. 185).

Nevertheless, the so-called "spirit of Davos" did not last long, as neither Greek public opinion nor Turkey responded accordingly, and eventually the initiative failed to resolve any of the substantive questions between the two countries. By the end of the 1980s, Greek–Turkish relations had returned to their depressingly familiar situation of mutually suspicious stand-off (Hale, 2013, p. 122). Furthermore, in the late 1980s, Turkey launched an impressive programme to modernise its armed forces (Tsakonas, 2010, p. 34).

Despite the fade-away of the Davos spirit, the rapprochement brought about some noteworthy achievements towards a viable *modus operandi* in the Aegean Sea. In May and September 1988, the Foreign Ministers of both countries Karolos Papoulias and Mesut Yilmaz, signed in Athens and Istanbul two memoranda.[42] Both parties commonly recognised the obligation to respect the sovereignty and the territorial integrity of each other and agreed on confidence-building measures: avoid interfering with smooth shipping and air traffic whenever the two countries conduct military exercises on the high seas and in the international airspace; avoid conducting military exercises during the peak tourist period (July–September); military and other activities carried out by the ships and aircraft of both countries on the high seas and international airspace would be conducted in accordance with the international law and international custom, instruments, rules, regulations and procedures, etc.

The opposition in Greece deplored the Papoulias–Yilmaz agreement, because it supposedly did not contain any reference to the sovereign rights of the two countries in the national waters and in the national airspace allowing the questioning of Greek national airspace rights (Rizas, 2000, pp. 100–104).

The fade-away of the Davos spirit was reflected in the CIA reports of that time. In April 1988, the CIA came to the conclusion that Greece and Turkey could hardly become US allies in a NATO engagement in southeast Europe. Furthermore, the recent culmination of the Greek–Turkish dispute and the possibility of a total disruption of NATO's Southern flank made once again obvious the eastern Mediterranean's strategic significance in the context of the East-West conflict. Therefore CIA officials underscored that there were cogent military reasons why Greek–Turkish political differences had to be resolved at any cost.[43]

By the end of the 1980s, the two countries continued to spend a large portion of their GDP on defence. According to CIA estimations, Greece was the only NATO country besides the USA to spend around

7% of its GDP on defence, whilst Turkey spent almost 4.8% of its GDP. The qualitative advantage Greece had developed in the late 1970s, when the US arms embargo against Turkey was still valid, evaporated in the 1980s. US and West-German aid coupled with the free-market orientation facilitated Turkey's domestic defence industries. Whilst Turkey was superior at the level of the ground forces, the Hellenic air force enjoyed a qualitative edge over the Turkish air force. Better equipment and a superior level of training gave Greece the potential to make Turkey pay a high price in casualties in the event of war. On balance, the Turkish navy, because of its modernisation programme, enjoyed a slight advantage over the Hellenic navy and this advantage would be evident, though not decisive, in an Aegean conflict. All in all, the sum of all Greek–Turkish military capabilities was rough parity, though it was steadily shifting toward Turkey. Turkish forces were stronger overall but had significant obligations elsewhere that precluded their total commitment against Greece in the Aegean.[44]

However, despite what political realists believe, the accumulation of weapons and the creation of a balance of power did not secure peace in the Aegean. On the contrary, it enhanced the risk of a warfare, since this situation could lead, as CIA officials very aptly and prophetically noted, any time to a conflict through miscalculation or overreaction to an anticipated incident. In the event of an accidental incident, the CIA further noticed that the political leadership in both countries would be under domestic pressure not to be the first to back down. This would reduce their manoeuvring room and increase the potential for a conflict that neither side actually needed.[45]

This appraisal turned out to be a self-fulfilling prophesy, since this conflict scenario repeated itself several times in the years that followed and unfortunately, remains still a strong possibility.

Notes

1 In 1978, even before official talks on the re-integration of Greece to NATO had started, Papandreou had tabled a question Parliament calling on the Greek Government to demand that NATO revises the Article 5 of the *North Atlantic Treaty* so that Greece would be protected in the event of an attack by a member state as well. US Department of State releases 2014: "Telegram from the US embassy in Athens to the Secretary of State in Washington, 25 January 1978".

2 PRO: FCO 9/4050: "Telegram of the British Embassy in Athens to the Foreign Office in London, Subject: the Soviet Union, Greece and the Alliance, 20 April 1983".

3 NATO archive: Document PO /81/123: "Secretary General's Greek-Turkish Relations Watching Brief, 27 November 1981".

4 NATO archive: Document PO /82/138: "Secretary General's Report on his Watching Brief to the December Ministerial Meeting of 1982, 30 November 1982".

5 PRO: FCO 9/4648: "British Secretary of State Report on the Relations Between Greece and Turkey, 6 February 1984".

6 NATO archive: Document PO /83/114: "Greek-Turkish Relations. Secretary General's Watching Brief to the December Ministerial Meeting of 1983, 2 December 1983".

7 CIA releases 2017: "Greece: Papandreou and the Military. An Intelligence Assessment (Secret), April 1983".

8 Archive of the Foreign Ministry of Former East Germany in Berlin: folder ZR 1532/84: "Report of the East German Embassy in Athens on the Greek-Turkish Conflict in the Aegean Sea 1982".

9 Political Archive of the Federal German Foreign Ministry: Folder 124894: "Conversation between the German Bundeskanzler Helmut Schmidt and the Greek Prime Minister in Bonn 19 June 1982 and Report on the Greek-German Relations, 1 June 1982"; Folder 124895 concerning the visit of Peter Corterier to Greece in Spring 1982.

10 Political Archive of the Federal German Foreign Ministry: folder 124896: "Internal Report of the German Federal Foreign Ministry on the Delivery Of 60 Fighter Planes of the Type Tornado, 2 February 1982" and "Internal Report of the Federal German Foreign Ministry on the Licence Approval on Weapons of Heckler and Koch to Greece 15 June 1982".

11 PRO: FCO 9/4648: "Report on the Upcoming Anglo-US Political and Military Talks on the 12 April 1984 on the Subject: Southern Flank Issues; Greece and Turkey (ii) 6 April 1984".

12 PRO: FCO 9/4648: "Telegram of the British Embassy in Athens to the Foreign Office and the diplomatic authorities in Ankara, Nicosia, Washington, 23 February 1984".

13 PRO: FCO 9/4648: "Report of the British Embassy in Athens on the Panther Incident, 21 March 1984"; "Exchange of Tele-Letters between Foreign Office and British Diplomatic Authorities in Ankara-Athens and Nicosia, March 1984".

14 PRO: FCO 9/4648: "Tele-Letter from the British Embassy in Ankara to the Foreign Office, 8 March 1984".

15 PRO: FCO 9/4648: "Telegram from the British Embassy in Athens (Subject: Greek-Turkish Relations), 28 March 1984".

16 PRO: FCO 9/4648: "Letter from the Hon DAG Asquith (South European Department) to Neilson 20 June 1984 about a Conversation with Petros Avierinos, Second Secretary at the Greek Embassy in London".

17 The Turkish Prime Minister Ozal seems to have been exasperated by purported Papandreou's references at the Panhellenic congress of his party to present areas of Turkey, including Istanbul, as being of concern for Hellenists PRO: FCO 9/4648: "Telegram from the British Embassy in Athens to the UK Diplomatic Missions in Athens to the UK diplomatic missions in NATO, May 30, 1984, Subject: Greece-Turkey Aircraft Violation"; "Telegram from the British Embassy in Ankara to the UK Diplomatic Missions in NATO and Boon 22 May 1984".

18 PRO: FCO 9/4648: "Telegrams from the British Embassy in Athens to the UK Mission to NATO and British Embassies in Washington and Ankara May 1984".

19 PRO: FCO 9/4648: "Southern European Department of the Foreign Office, Reports from M.R.H. Jenkins, 19 March 1984, and from Asquith, 23 March 1984".

20 PRO: FCO 9/4648: "Lemnos: Greek-Turkish Dispute in the Aegean, Confidential Report for Internal Use in the Foreign Office, DCR 11, 1984".

21 In Turkey the respective straits are called "Turkish Straits".

22 PRO: FCO 9/4648: "Telegram from the UK Delegate to NATO to the British Embassies in Ankara, Athens and Nicosia".

23 PRO: FCO 9/4648: "Telegrams from the British Ambassador in Ankara to the Foreign Office in May 1984".

24 PRO: FCO 9/4648: "Telegrams from the British Embassy in Ankara to the Foreign Office in London, Washington, Athens and UK Mission to NATO, November 21, 22 and 23, 1984"; PRO: FCO 9/5737: "Telegrams from the UK delegation in NATO to the Foreign Office November 1987".

25 PRO: FCO 9/4648: "Telegrams from the British Embassy in Ankara to the Foreign Office in London, Washington, Athens and UK mission to NATO, November 21, 22 and 23, 1984".

26 PRO: FCO 9/4648: "Report from the British Consulate in Istanbul to Ankara on Military Perspectives in the Aegean 13 March 1984".

27 PRO: FCO 9/4648: "Southern European Department of the Foreign Office, Asquith's Draft Report on Lemnos and the Greek-Turkish Maritime Dispute, 11 May 1984".

28 PRO: FCO 9/4648: "Telegrams from the UK Mission to NATO to the British Embassies Ankara, Athens and the Foreign Office, 22 and 23 November 1984".

29 The delimitation of national airspace claimed by Greece is unique, as it does not coincide with the boundary of the territorial waters. Pursuant to the Decree of 6 September 1931 in conjunction with the Law 5017/1931 it extends to 10 nautical miles. A country's airspace rights usually coincide with its territorial sea rights. Greece claims a 6-mile sea limit. Therefore, other countries, including the United States, recognise Greek airspace as only 6 miles (US Congressional Research Service's report for US Congress, 1997, p. 1).

30 PRO: FCO 9/4648: "Southern European Department of the Foreign Office, Asquith Draft Report on Lemnos and the Greek-Turkish Maritime Dispute, May 11, 1984".

31 PRO: FCO 9/5737: "Internal paper of the Foreign Office ahead of the Visit of the Greek Foreign Minister in Landon in November 1987".

32 PRO: FCO 9/5079: "Report of the British Embassy in Ankara to the Foreign and Commonwealth Office, Subject: UK/Turkey/Greece, 21 November 1985".

33 PRO: FCO 9/5079: "Internal Confidential Report of the Foreign Office on Greece/Turkey Relations: Illustrative Action in the Event of Incidents in the Aegean, 5 December 1985".

34 PRO: FCO 9/5441: "Telegrams from the British Embassy in Greece and the UK Delegation to NATO to the Foreign Office, September and October 1986".

35 CIA Releases 2017: "Greece: Directorate of Intelligence 4 September 1986, Greece-Turkey-Cyprus: Trouble Ahead?"

36 CIA Releases 2017: "Greece: Directorate of Intelligence 4 September 1986, Greece-Turkey-Cyprus: Trouble Ahead?".

37 NATO Archive: Document CZ MT887l8: "Note by the Secretary General, Report on the Situation in the Mediterranean, October 1987–April 1988, 29th April 1988, Composition and Strength of the Soviet Mediterranean Squadron and Other Mediterranean Naval Activities".

38 PRO: FCO 9/5717: "Telegram from the British Embassy in Athens to the Foreign Office, April 1987".

39 PRO: FCO 9/5718: "Telegrams from the British Embassies in Ankara and Athens to the Foreign Office, June 1987".

40 In Turkey's view, Greece has been violating the status of Dodecanese Islands, to which Rhodes belongs, by militarising them since the 1960s in contravention of its contractual obligations emanating from the *Paris Treaty* of 1947. Greece maintains that it only retains a National Guard presence there in accordance with the provisions of the 1947 *Peace Treaty*, while Turkey, as not signatory state to this *Treaty*, cannot raise any claims.

41 NATO Archive: Document C-R (88) 59: "Summary Record of a Meeting of the Council held at the NATO Headquarters, Brussels, 22nd November 1988".

42 Memorandum of Understanding between Greece and Turkey signed in May 1988. Available from https://www.mfa.gov.tr/site_media/html/aegean-sea-reference-documents-1.pdf; Guidelines for the Preventions of Accidents and Incidents on the High Seas and International Airspace signed in September 1988. Available at: https://www.mfa.gov.tr/site_media/html/aegean-sea-reference-documents-2.pdf

43 CIA Releases 2017: "Greece: Memorandum on the Mediterranean Workshop, 28 May 1987".

44 CIA Releases 2017: "Memorandum on the Military Balance between Greece and Turkey; How it Stands, Where It Is Headed, What It Means, June 1988".

45 Ibidem.

References

Primary Sources

Public Record Office (PRO)

Archive of the Foreign Ministry of the Former East Germany in Berlin

CIA Releases 2017

Memorandum of Understanding between Greece and Turkey, signed in May 1988. Available from www.mfa.gov.tr/site_media/html/aegean-sea-reference-documents-1.pdf

Guidelines for the Preventions of Accidents and Incidents on the High Seas and International Airspace, signed in September 1988. Available from www.mfa.gov.tr/site_media/html/aegean-sea-reference-documents-2.pdf

NATO Archive

Secondary Sources

Coufoudakis, V., 1993. PASOK and Greek-Turkish Relations. In Clogg, R. (ed.), *Greece, 1981–89. The Populist Decade* (pp. 167–180). Houndmills, Basingstoke: The Macmillan Press.

Hale, W., 2013. *Turkish Foreign Policy since 1774* (3rd ed.). London and New York: Routledge.

Kollias, Ch., 1995. The effects of external security considerations on defence expenditure in the context of Greek-Turkish bilateral relations. *Bogazici Journal Review of Social, Economic and Administrative Studies*, 9 (1), 135–147.

Lioliou, A., 1999. *On the resilience of perceptual states in foreign policy shaping or the antinomy of reversibly in patterns of foreign policy behaviour: a case study on Greek socialist foreign policy decision-making during the time-period 1981–1989*. Thesis submitted for the degree of Ph.D., University of Reading.

Papacosma, V., 2001. Greece and NATO: A nettlesome relationship. In: G. Schmidt (ed.), *A History of NATO – The First Fifty Years* (pp. 359–374). Basingstoke, Hampshire: Palgrave.

Richter, H., 2021. *The conflicts of the Aegean in the 20th century*. Peleus Studien zur Geschichte Griechenlands und Zyperns Band 113. Wiesbaden: Harrassowitz Verlag.

Rizas, S., 2000. *Apo tin Krisi stin ifesi. O Konstantinos Mitsotakis kai I politiki tiw proseggisis Elladas-Tourkias [From the crisis to the détente. Konstantinos Mitsotakis and Greece's Rapprochement Policy Towards Turkey]*. Athens: Papazisis Publisher.

Roubatis, G., 1986. *Anatomia ton Ellinonatoikon Scheseon [Anatomy of the Greece-NATO relations]*. In G. Valinakis and P. Kitsos (Eds), *Ellinika Amyntika Provlimata [Greece's Defence Problems]*. Athens: Papazisis Publisher.

Stearns, M., (1992). *Entangled Allies. US policy toward Greece, Turkey and Cyprus*. New York: Council on Foreign Relations Press.

Stergiou, A., & Kollias, Chr., 2018. Between pragmatism and rhetoric: A critical assessment of Greece's defence and foreign policy in the 1980s in light of new primary sources, *Journal for Southeast European and Black Sea Studies*, 18 (4), 549–571.

Stergiou, A., 2021. *Greece's Ostpolitik. Dealing With the "Devil"*. Contribution to the International Relations. Switzerland AG: Springer Nature.

Stergiou, A., 2022. *The Greek-Turkish Maritime Dispute. Resisting the Future*. Switzerland AG: Springer Nature.

Tsakonas, P., 2010. *The Incomplete Breakthrough in Greek–Turkish Relations. Grasping Greece's Socialization Strategy*. New York: Palgrave Macmillan.

Tsardanidis, C., 2002. Greek foreign policy since the World War II. In P. Liargovas (ed.), *Greece: Economics, Social and Political Issues* (pp. 237–249). New York: Nova Science Publishers.

Vinocur, J., 1984. Allies mistrustful of Greece. Said to bypass it in decisions. *New York Times*, 10 June 1984.

US Congressional Research Service's report for US Congress (1997). *Greece and Turkey: Aegean Issues – Background and Recent Developments.* Washington: US Congress.

Veremis, Th., 1993. Defence and security policies under PASOK. In R. Clogg (ed.), *Greece, 1981–89. The Populist Decade* (pp. 181–189). Houndmills, Basingstoke: Macmillan Press.

Conclusions

The years 1973–1974 were a watershed period in the eastern Mediterranean and a test for NATO coherence. First, a series of tensions between two NATO members making up the sensitive south-east flank of the alliance, Greece and Turkey, on the legitimacy of hydrocarbon explorations in the north Aegean marked the advent of the intractable Aegean dispute that has continued ever since. Second, the culmination of old national and political rivalries and antagonisms between the two living communities in Cyprus, the Greek and the Turkish Cypriots, as well as between the supporters and the Greek junta-backed opponents of the President of the Cyprus Republic Makarios, ended up with the Turkish invasion of the island and its de facto division. Both developments also raised the possibility of a high-scale military conflict between Greece and Turkey, which threatened to dismantle for good NATO's presence in the region.

The Aegean dispute with its various aspects (militarisation of the eastern Aegean islands, delimitation of the continental shelf, airspace and air traffic control, as well as the issue of the territorial waters, believed in general to emerge in the mid-1990s) is thoroughly studied in this book. In particular, the study has endeavoured to explain why the two countries came on the verge of war in the wake of attempted exploration activities over commercially insignificant oil deposits. Despite the then wild speculations of tremendous oil reserves in the northern Aegean, the overall dispute was not about energy but about sovereignty. Turkey's assertive policy in the Aegean should rather be attributed to the belief that it was treated unfairly by its neighbour due to its exclusion from the development of energy discoveries. Therefore, it was primarily aimed at undermining Greece's sovereignty in disputed areas.

The Cyprus crisis in the summer of 1974 is analysed in this study through a new prism and runs counter to many scholarly

DOI: 10.4324/9781003350033-7

contributions to the respective events. More precisely, it is argued that the division of Cyprus was not the result of a long-term plan by the main stakeholders in the conflict, NATO, the United States or Britain since 1954, as many scholars have argued, though all these bear some responsibility for what happened in Cyprus in 1974.

The causes of the division go back to a much earlier time, and they are only partially the result of the British colonial *divide-and-rule policy* as has been asserted by various scholars. It is indisputable that the UK followed a divisive course in Cyprus, especially during the war of independence during 1955–1959. However, the seeds of division were inherent in the Cypriot society regardless of the British policy. The consolidation of Greek and Turkish nationalism on the island, mainly through education and the mutual suspicion between the two communities since the early 20th century, had created a deep rift between the two communities that came to the surface on various occasions. The study shows that the two communities had diametrically opposed political aspirations long before the 1950s, when the British colonial authorities decided to exploit the two nationalisms expressed either in the *Enosis* ideology (union with Greece) for the Greek Cypriots or primarily in the continuation of the British colonialism or more rarely *Taksim* (union with Turkey) for the Turkish Cypriots. The creation of a state based on a constitution that celebrated the institutionalisation of ethnicity in 1960 only compounded the already strained relations between the two communities and between Greece and Turkey which proved to be incompetent or unwilling to control the hardliners, leading inevitably to the war in 1974.

Yet, NATO's response to the events in Cyprus was inert and against its role as a security provider in the wider region. The US's and UK's roles in the conflict were also inconsistent with their obligations or their declared commitment to the territorial integrity and independence of the Cyprus Republic. All three acted during the dramatic events in July and August 1974, as if the crisis were not of their concern at all, whereas there is much evidence to suggest that Kissinger and London approved or connived the Turkish invasion. The inherited difficulties in an active engagement of NATO on Cyprus that would have to act beyond its ambit and practically against Turkey, a member-state of the alliance, should not exonerate the "alliance inertia".

In order to exert pressure on NATO to force Turkey to withdraw its occupying soldiers from the northern half of Cyprus, the new democratic Greek government decided to withdraw its forces from NATO's military command structure in August 1974. This was a seminal move, albeit not a well-thought-out one and strategically wrong, and could not be paralleled with the analogous French case in the 1960s. The country was faced with security challenges, for which it was not well-equipped. Since the strategic damage inflicted on the south-eastern flank of NATO from Greece's absence was tremendous, Athens' decision to seek re-integration into NATO a few years later was well-received by all NATO members except Turkey. Thus, Greece's return to the alliance turned out to be a very thorny and complicated issue requiring hard and arduous negotiations with NATO that tried to maintain a balance between Turkey's categorical refusal to consent to Greece's return and the deteriorating Aegean dispute.

Turkey, on its part, tried to use the negotiations as a means of achieving its objective to extend its operational control to the West, namely into areas of responsibility, which were under Greek responsibility until 1974. Athens, however, accepted nothing else as a return to the pre-1974 arrangements of operational control in the Aegean Sea. Eventually, in October 1980, the re-integration of Greece was made possible on the basis of a proposal that became known as the *Rogers Plan* and within a context of "constructive ambiguity" regarding the key items of contention that continued to fuel tensions among the two countries in the next years.

The expected stabilisation of NATO's sensitive south-eastern flank never came. On the contrary, NATO was embroiled in the Greek–Turkish maritime dispute, for which Athens and Ankara constantly exerted pressure on their NATO allies to take sides. NATO's everyday operations were continuously disrupted by issues like the inclusion or exclusion of Lemnos from the alliance's military exercises, the distribution of resources to the two countries, etc., forcing the organisation to continually come up with new strategies to maintain its functionality in the region.

For NATO the permanent, recurring challenge was finding the ideal balance of rewards and threats to constrain its two allies from fighting each other without losing either of them. Sometimes, NATO allies appeared inert or indifferent towards the Greek–Turkish conflict, sometimes as strictly neutral, while occasionally they engaged in finding conciliatory solutions and bridging the differences between the two allies. Given the deep-routed divergences between the two nations and the strengthening of Cyprus' division, in all cases the alliance failed to endear itself to the Greek, Turkish and Cypriot peoples. NATO remained permanently unpopular in the societies of the three countries, in some cases even less popular than the Soviet Union! The archival documents clearly show that both the United States' and the United Kingdom's experts meticulously and thoroughly studied the legal aspects of the dispute and were fully aware of which argument brought up by each side was valid or tendentious and sensationalist. Nonetheless, both NATO as an organisation and the individual NATO states, followed a course of strict neutrality shaped by their intention not to get involved in the Greek–Turkish conflict. Undoubtedly, this is the usual practice in international relations. However, by shirking responsibility and avoiding wading into the real causes of the Greek–Turkish conflict the allies simply let a problem get bigger and bigger, undermining the coherence of the alliance. They solely became active only whenever a severe crisis arose and tensions culminated. This, however, not only turned out to be shortsighted, but also ineffective.

The consolidation of the division in Cyprus especially after the unilateral and internationally non-recognised declaration of the establishment of the so-called Turkish Republic of Northern Cyprus in the Turkish-controlled area exacerbated tensions in the eastern Mediterranean. In 1987, tensions reached a critical point that almost resulted in a war that was averted literally at the very last minute by Peter Carington, Secretary General of NATO, who stepped in to avert the disaster. The crisis was followed up by a détente that was transformed into a rapprochement in 1988. In the context of the rapprochement, for the very first time efforts were undertaken not only to initiate confidence-building measures and to settle the outstanding issues but also to erase some of the causes of the conflict, the nationalistic narratives penetrated the schoolbooks in both countries, etc. The undertaking failed for reasons that had made similar efforts in the 1970s to fail. Once again, domestic opposition and the press in both countries, regardless of their political and ideological orientation, put serious obstacles in this process. They took advantage of the deep-seated mistrust between the two sides, sullied the situation by painting the politicians carrying out the agreements as traitors, and ultimately made it difficult to find long-term, viable solutions to the fundamental Greek-Turkish bilateral problems. Concerning the role of the press and the opposition in both countries, the most tragic aspect is that, as yet, nothing has changed in this direction.

Index

Aegean Army 66, 108, 109
Aegean Sea, dispute over 48, 65–66;
  Britain on 50–51, 56–57; Candarli
  ship issue and 55–56; Cyprus
  Crisis and 58; domestic politics
  impacting 60; exploratory drilling
  by Turkey and 49–50; Geneva
  Convention on 52–53, 63–64;
  International Court of Justice on
  61–63; Joint Communiqué of the
  ministers' meeting and 59–60, 63;
  minorities issue and 54–55; UN
  Security Council on 61; United
  States on 52, 56, 59, 62, 64
Agnew, S. 72
airspace and territorial waters,
  violations of 104–105
Akiman, N. 111
Allied Land Forces South-Eastern
  Europe (LANDSOUTHEAST)
  82
Androutsopoulos 48
anti-Americanism 6n4, 94
anti-Hellenic culture 16
Aphrodite plan 33
Arapakis, P. 29
Attila Line 20, 87
Averof, E. 28, 36, 74, 77, 83n2, 89

balanced approach, concept of 27
balance of power 4, 37, 60, 75, 88,
  116
Berne Declaration (1976) 111
bicommunality, issue of 14, 16, 21,
  55, 90

Bilge 60
Bitsios, D. 59, 62, 89
bizonality, issue of 90
Bosporus Straits 106
Boyatt, T. 27

Callaghan, J. 30
Candarli ship, issue of 55
Carrington, P. 6, 95, 108, 125
Carter, J. 62, 79, 81
Chorafas, A. 24
CIA 18, 40n21, 57, 58, 64, 66, 115,
  116
Committee for Turkish Affairs 12
Conference on Security and
  Cooperation in Europe (CSCE)
  95
Craig, I. 25
Cyprus conflict (1974): *Enosis* and
  16, 21; military junta and 33–36;
  NATO and 17, 21–23, 25, 29;
  origins of 2–3; Soviet Union on
  28–29; United Kingdom on 9–13,
  30–31; *see also individual entries*
Cyprus question evolution 87
Cyprus Working Group 22

Davos Declaration (1988) 113–114
Davou 79
Demirel 59, 60, 62
Denktash, R. 10, 14, 21, 89, 90, 91,
  93–95, 98n12
Denver (company) 48
Dodecanese islands 109, 114,
  119n40

For Product Safety Concerns and Information please contact our EU
representative GPSR@taylorandfrancis.com
Taylor & Francis Verlag GmbH, Kaufingerstraße 24, 80331 München, Germany